ROTISSERIE BASEBALL: PLAYING FOR FUN

By John Benson
and Randall Baron

Devyn Press, Inc.
Louisville, Kentucky

Cover design by Richard Bram and Grady Long

Rotisserie League Baseball® is a federally registered
trademark of the Rotisserie League Baseball Association, Inc.,
370 7th Ave. #312, New York, NY 10001, 212-629-4036.

Printed in the United States of America.

Devyn Press, Inc.
3600 Chamberlain Lane, Suite 230
Louisville, KY 40241

ISBN 0-910791-86-4

TABLE OF CONTENTS

DEDICATION

*To Roberto Clemente, who would have
been a great Rotisserie player.*

ACKNOWLEDGEMENTS

Special thanks to the following who have been helpful to the co-authors over the past few years:

LARY BUMP
HARRY CONOVER
BILL CUNNINGHAM
MIKE DALECKI
PETE DECOURSEY
JOHN DEWAN
PETER GOLENBOCK
BILL GRAY
JERRY HEATH

GARY LEVY
TIM McQUAY
GLEN WAGGONER
JOHN WALLWORK
PAUL WHITE
JACK "HOT BYTE" WILLIAMS
ROB WOOD
DON ZMINDA

Jude Goodwin-Hanson for her unique cartoons.

Betty Mattison for her typesetting. Ralph "The Buffalo" Letizia and Mike Mangeot for their proofreading/editing.

Special thanks to Greg Ambrosius and Kit Kiefer for their gracious assistance throughout this book.

Some of this material has appeared in Fantasy Baseball Magazine; Krause Publications owns perpetual, non-exclusive rights for various essays.

JOHN'S PREFACE

If you write a book about bridge or chess, you don't have to include a long explanation defining the game. Even if your reader is a complete novice, you can outline the rules quickly and proceed to the fun parts. You can also depend on your reader to know SOMETHING about any game that has been around for hundreds of years.

But imagine a book about baseball strategy, aimed at readers who have never played the game and never even seen it played: "Well, you start with a guy throwing a ball to another guy, and a third guy swings at the ball as it goes by, and if he hits it, he runs, and seven other guys chase after the ball . . ." The author could become lost in detail, long before he got into subjects like the double switch and the suicide squeeze.

Another difficulty could arise if you tried to tell people why they should play baseball: "Well, it's fun, you know, and good healthy exercise, or it could involve lots of beer and hot dogs if that's what you like, and you make friends . . ." Considering the existential appeal of baseball, which grows with experience, it is a miracle that people in faraway places like Europe have taken only 150 years to give the game a try during the 1990's. It is very hard to explain to a foreigner (or any of the uninitiated) why the game is worthwhile.

Rotisserie baseball is a new game. We don't have a century of history. We don't have a huge body of literature. Most of the educated people in the world have never heard of Rotisserie baseball and very few know how to play. Many of the people who know a little about Rotisserie games, including some of sports media professionals, are remarkably uninformed on many of the key aspects. There is a shortage of good information and a surplus of misinformation.

In the face of these problems, starting a Rotisserie book isn't easy. If you don't have any interest in the subject, there isn't too much I can say to get you interested, so I won't put a big effort into trying to grab your attention. Of course, you may have been interested in the subject long before you ever picked up this book, so you don't want a long sales pitch, anyway.

Rotisserie baseball, like art, music, literature, and astrophysics, has the power to make people happy. If you enjoy baseball, you probably possess the deep, subconscious motivations that will make you love Rotisserie, without much urging from me or anyone else. If you are one of those people who check the stats and standings at least once a week, you are half way to playing the game already.

RANDY'S PREFACE

We Are The Champions Of The World

As a sports fan, I am sure some of your fondest memories resulted from when your team won the championship. Whether it was the Dodgers winning the World Series, the Steelers winning the Super Bowl or the University of Louisville winning the NCAA Championship, these victories made you feel like you were part of the team. Your celebration could not have been anymore frenzied if you had been a team member. In fact, even though you were hundreds or thousands of miles away from the ultimate victory, it still felt like you personally had a hand in the triumph.

Rotisserie Baseball takes the ecstasy one step further! It really is your team. You are the owner, general manager, manager, third base coach and press secretary, all rolled into one. When your team captures the league title, the pride is overwhelming. The other owners can blame their misfortune on your good luck, but deep down you know that it was your decisions that made the difference.

On the other hand, if you experience the agony of defeat rather than the thrill of victory, you will know that it was your miscalculations that kept the team from winning the pennant. Although you were not on the field personally, you have the same feeling of achievement or frustration as the major league front office personnel.

Even if you do not win, the thrill of being part of a pennant race is the ultimate excitement. In our Cardinal Sin (National) and Wildcat Sin (American) Leagues, the race has come down to the final day every year and in most instances to the final game. I hope that your leagues can be this competitive and that our book (*Playing For Fun*) will play a large part in your enjoyment.

On the other hand, you would probably rather crush the other teams and have your league clinched by the All-Star break. Then you're a perfect candidate for Volume 2, *Playing For Blood*. Just make sure the other owners don't have a copy.

INTRODUCTION
AMERICA'S GREATEST GAME

> *"Next to religion, baseball has furnished a greater impact on American life than any other institution."*
> — *President Herbert Hoover*

If baseball is the national pasttime, Rotisserie baseball is the new national passion. Simply stated, Rotisserie is a contest to see who can choose the best players. The elegant parts include how you pick the players and what happens after you have them.

There is something uniquely American about assembling a baseball team. A hundred years ago, anyone with enough time and money could field a world class team and watch them play. Soon, however, professional leagues and contracts locked up all the best players. Today, you need something like $100 million just to think about drafting and managing your own major leaguebaseball team.

Fortunately, there are some less expensive ways to test your player-selection skills. Youngsters can assemble fantastic teams using baseball cards as markers: Cecil Fielder at first base, Ryne Sandberg at second, and so forth. (If the card enthusiasts are serious, they can look at the stats on their cards, and total up the numbers of their imaginary rosters for comparison.) Various tabletop and computer games, such as Pursue the Pennant and APBA leagues, begin with a pre-season draft. All kinds of office pools and homemade lotteries revolve around questions like which hitter will slug the most home runs, and which pitcher will win the most games each year, suggesting various possibilities for roster-based contests.

When a writer tries to tell people about Rotisserie leagues, the usual problem is getting bogged down in details. The game has huge dimensions. Focusing on any one aspect too early will obscure the big picture. The game is built around a full baseball season, so it takes about seven months to play. There are a thousand professional players who might be a factor in the big leagues in any one year, so there is a long list of possible rostercandidates. These big dimensions are one of the qualities that makes the game so interesting.

If you like simple games, stay with tic-tac-toe or connect-the-dots. There are some simplified variations of Rotisserie baseball, but all of them are multifaceted. To get an idea what we're dealing with, consider the following metaphors . . .

- a horse race with a thousand thoroughbreds running eight heats simultaneously on the same track;
- poker with fifteen players at the table, and twenty packs of cards in use;
- backgammon played on 26 boards, each covering several acres; and
- chess with a thousand pieces that all move differently.

If you find these images stimulating rather than repulsive, you have the potential to be a great Rotisserian.

Rotisserie baseball leads a phenomenal surge in the popularity of games that create imaginary baseball teams on paper. The participants become "owners," and each group of rival roster-builders is called a league. They meet in April to select their players for the coming year. The winner is decided by totaling the actual player performances through October and seeing whose players did the best in certain predetermined statistical categories.

There is widespread use of the term "fantasy league" to describe Rotisserie and other contests that put real players and real statistics onto rosters that exist only for the people who create them. It may be a fantasy to see Will Clark, Barry Larkin and Delino Deshields combining in a common effort, but there is nothing unreal about the competition to assemble and manage these rosters. If Rotisserie is "fantasy baseball," then chess is "fantasy warfare," and horse racing is "fantasy cavalry." The people who play these games are not pretending anything; they

9

are simply trying to win.

Be aware that the terms, "fantasy" and "Rotisserie" baseball, are sometimes used interchangeably by enthusiasts. This can be confusing, since "fantasy" is a general term for any statistical competition and "Rotisserie" is a specific set of rules. We prefer to use the word "Rotisserie" to describe the game, because we recommend these rules and variations of them to you. They are logical, workable and enjoyable for most leagues.

Rotisserie League Baseball (a federally registered trademark of the RLBA, Inc.) is named for a New York restaurant, La Rotisserie Francaise, where the game's founding fathers launched their original competition in 1980. The restaurant is long gone, so don't expect a cabbie to take you there during your next visit to the Big Apple; you would have a better chance of finding Ebbets Field. The Rotisserie genesis has been documented by Glen Waggoner, Dan Okrent and others in their landmark work ROTISSERIE LEAGUE BASEBALL (Bantam Books). Today, that volume is the bible for the league's elegant rules and methods, and is an indispensable annual guide to the frontiers of Rotisserie science.

1ST INNING

GETTING STARTED

> *"The team that gets off to a good start*
> *wins pennants."*
> — *John McGraw*

THE LINEUP

⚾ What format should your league use?

⚾ How do you form a league or find an existing one?

⚾ What decisions are involved in running a league?

⚾ How much time does it take?

The major decision you have to make when getting into a pick-your-players competition is the question of whether to use the Rotisserie format or follow a different method. You can, follow some of the Rotisserie rules and make changes in selected areas. Some of the alternative games are like Rotisserie and some are radically different.

If you follow Rotisserie rules, you will get various benefits:

(1) **Following Rotisserie rules will give you the maximum benefit from the many books and publications that discuss the game,** especially the materials covering player valuation and "fantasy prices." If you don't follow Rotisserie methods, these books will still be useful, but their usefulness will be limited.

(2) **Following Rotisserie guidelines will allow you to compare notes with people in other leagues,** share common experiences, and make friends with people outside your own league.

11

Give considerable thought to the makeup of your league.
A Rotisserie league should have a healthy mix
of personalities.

(3) **The Rotisserie League Baseball Association provides a national organization** with a standard set of rules revised each year. RLBA represents the cumulative and progressive thinking of the game's greatest minds.

(4) **The RLBA method is a realistic simulation** of the decisions that have to be made by real baseball executives.

If you decide to adopt the Rotisserie format with no variations, there aren't many decisions that you have to make. You can just buy the official book, Rotisserie League Baseball, find enough people to start a league and commence playing. Much as we admire the Rotisserie formula, however, there are some alternatives worth considering. Some people, especially beginners, may want to try something "easier" for their first season and others will have variations they personally prefer. We will give you rules options throughout this book.

PRIVATE OR PUBLIC

The first decision you will have to make is whether to form your own "private" league or to join one of the "public" leagues available to anyone.

There are five basic activities involved in forming a private league.

(1) **You need to form the league** with an appropriate number of individual participants.

(2) **Write the rules [NEVER play without written rules].**

(3) **Administer the league during the season,** making rules interpretations, recording player acquisitions and changes, managing the league treasury, and handling problems like inactive owners, dropouts and arguments.

(4) **Keep the league standings** and statistics during the season, and issue reports periodically.

(5) **Provide a league social secretary** to help keep everyone interested and entertained

---

You can hire a professional fantasy baseball service company to handle any or all of the above chores. Many leagues choose a "full service" organization, such as Bill James Fantasy Baseball, to handle all of these tasks. Most leagues eventually decide to hire a professional stat service (see Chapter 10 for the list), but many of them keep all the other duties for members to perform themselves. If you have a group that wants to play inexpensively, you can do everything yourself, including the stat keeping.

If you are one individual searching for competition, the numerous commercial play-by-mail, play-by-phone, and play-by-computer organizations will put you in a public league and get you started (See Chapter 10 for the list). One of the major benefits of the public leagues is that you don't need to know anyone to join and have fun. You can make friends after you start playing.

Most people get into a fantasy league initially because a friend or acquaintance invites them. Many leagues are built around a close-knit group of friends or co-workers. Rotisserie rules encourage league members to interact heavily. By the time you've been through one annual cycle together, you will know each other all too well, even if you were mere acquaintances at the outset.

The social aspect of the game should never be underestimated. **The play-by-mail, public access leagues perform a valuable service, but my advice is to form your own group, if you can possibly find enough people.** You can always change the rules to accommodate a smaller number of competitors (see Chapter 2).

One caution: don't go around twisting arms to make people play. A disinterested competitor is no use to any league and unenthusiastic people can cause a great deal of harm, unintentional or otherwise. When the last-place owner loses interest in July, and gives all his good players to his best friend before disappearing to Cape Cod or Reno, people will contemplate mayhem.

As a private group, your league administers itself. You make the rules, you enforce them strictly or haphazardly, and you even change the rules in midseason (something we never advise) if it suits you. You can hire a professional stat service to help you keep score or do it yourself. Most importantly, you will decide who's in your league and who's out.

Many great friendships have been formed (or broken) as a result of Rotisserie league competition. **Give utmost attention to the selection of your league members.** Your league will run much smoother if you exclude everyone who has been known to lie, steal, or belch in an elevator. Just like a regular poker group, a Rotisserie league needs a healthy mix of good personalities. You want some cold, calculating types; some romantic, wishful thinkers; optimists and pessimists; some egotists and some insecure types.

The one thing you don't want is people who are short on social conscience. Dropping out of a league on draft day, for example, will throw ten innocent individuals into the darkest pit in Hell, as they suffer through the question of what to do with the abandoned roster. If you know someone who might drop a commitment suddenly, don't tell them about Rotisserie baseball.

TIME MANAGEMENT

One of the most common objections to joining a Rotisserie league is the time consumption factor. People often get in trouble with their friends and spouses when they get wrapped up in their Rotisserie team. The crimes include reading box scores day and night, carrying a transistor radio everywhere, and tying up the home (or office) telephone with trade negotiations. Falling asleep on the couch while watching the late-late ESPN wrap-up will not help you get along with your spouse or your boss.

It is a fact that most people get deeply absorbed, but it isn't necessary to invest forty hours a week to have fun. We play pretty seriously ourselves and would say that five hours a week is enough to do a decent job of roster management in most leagues. Much depends on the style of your league.

You can easily design a league where there is nothing to do during the baseball season. You can pick your players in April and check back in October to see whose roster has the best stats. Most likely, you will find that you want to replace disabled players with healthy bodies and you will feel the urge to grab hot prospects when they get promoted to the major leagues during the summer. These roster transactions are the life-blood of most Rotisserie leagues, but it's a free country. You can play with limited activity if time is a major concern.

Even if you get hooked, there are ways to keep your life under control, or at least to appear under control. Get a separate phone for your league conversations. Tell your boss that things are a little rough at home and tell your spouse that things are tough at work. Stay late at the office frequently, spending the time to read box scores. Keep your newspaper folded open to the stats page and place it in a drawer so that you can simply close the drawer if anyone comes in. If you use a computer, put your league info on a spreadsheet, and put some real work at the top of the spreadsheet; if your boss appears suddenly, just push the "home" key, and the real work will appear on your computer screen. A budget worksheet labeled "departmental cost reduction ideas" is my favorite content.

If you decide to join a public access league, or if you join a previously-existing private league, most of the administrative chores and decisions will be handled for you. As a new member of a private league, at some point you will probably be asked to vote on rules changes. Even as a novice, you can make some intelligent contributions.

At your organizational meeting (or by mail or phone, if that's how your league operates), ask questions about existing rules and proposed changes. One good method is to put the burden of proof on people who want to change the existing rules. Don't let anyone impose a change if their only argument is: "Try it for a year, and if it doesn't work, we can drop it next year." The "try it" people usually haven't thought through the consequences of their new rules.

Start with the question, "What's wrong with the current rule?" Anyone who wants to change something should have a valid complaint about a real problem that actually occurred during the previous season. Obviously, the solution should address that problem without creating a new world of difficulties. If the only anecdotes are about problems that MIGHT have arisen, that means the rules actually worked last year and you should be very cautious about making any changes. In many cases adding examples and interpretations will solve most of the problems that came up. We are generally in favor of writing longer rules with more detailed explanations, especially when people have questions that aren't addressed specifically. The less you leave for interpretation later, the better your league will operate.

If you have any questions about forming a league or finding a league, there are some excellent resources. Chapter 10 includes a long list with details. The best resource, as we will keep telling you, is to call 900-773-7526, and talk to John Benson personally for advice and answers.

Finally, if you are going to accept the responsibilities of league secretary or commissioner, you will need this book's companion volume, ROTISSERIE BASEBALL: PLAYING FOR BLOOD.

SO NOW YOU'RE IN A LEAGUE — WELCOME TO THE CLUB!

Whichever path you follow, starting your own new league, joining an existing private league, or going solo (or with friends) into a professionally-administered league, you can have some fun before you even get to the competitive part. Sit back and think about some of the benefits you are soon to enjoy.

Playing Rotisserie will increase your knowledge of baseball. Recently one of the ESPN broadcasters reflected on the schedule that had him visiting every major league city and seeing every major league team. "Not since I was a boy," he said, "with a box full of well-worn baseball cards, have I been so familiar with every player on every team. This job really has an astounding impact on your knowledge of rosters and player personnel!" The same benefit comes to everyone who experiences a Rotisserie season.

On draft day, you must be familiar with every name, at least to the extent of having an opinion of every player's value. During the season, you will watch your own players intensely and you should also be aware of the players on the other rosters. If you play half-way seriously, you will be acutely aware of players who come and go during the season or deliver surprising performances.

John B.: In my previous life, I was responsible for the care and feeding (and occasional discipline) of a 550-person sales force scattered around the country. In this job, I had occasion to travel frequently and I visited just about every major league city. Most of the sales managers had tickets for ball games, so it worked well. Wherever I went, we had a pleasant topic of conversation, to fill in the gaps between discussions of where the revenue had gone.

There is no better way to establish rapport in the U.S. of A. than to start talking local baseball with local people. Casual fans usually have a knowledge of their hometown team, but they don't know much about other teams. If you go to Dallas and raise questions about the trade that landed Rafael Palmeiro, or go to Seattle and ask about Harold Reynolds' base-stealing performance, or go anywhere and ask about the local versions of Joe Bimbleman and Carlos Gonzalez, you are going to make friends and influence people.

People will give you credit for being a Renaissance Man and a great modern thinker if you know the lineup of their local baseball team. The only possibility of someone not being impressed is if they play Rotisserie, too. And in that case, you can open a whole new world of esoteric conversation about long-term contracts, disabilities, and prices paid on draft day. Find another Rotisserian, and you have instant friendship that rivals the door-opening, "Hello, Hiram!"

In your own hometown, your league forms an invisible bond between you and your fellow competitors. At work, you have a new reason to visit people in other departments. After you join a Rotisserie league, you have all kinds of one-on-one, closed-door meetings. Don't tell anyone that you are talking trading Will Clark for David Justice! Let people think you are part of some new task force that reports directly to the President. Even your boss will be afraid to press for details when he sees the breadth of your new responsibilities, whatever they may be.

On a serious note, some companies justifiably get concerned when Rotisserie conversations take up half of a person's workday. Indeed, some people have been disciplined, or even fired, for too much play and not enough work. We never advocate dropping your responsibilities, but we believe too many uninformed managers simply don't see the benefits of a Rotisserie league in the workplace. Softball teams, charities, blood drives, golf outings and company picnics are officially condoned and even promoted as proper use of "work" time. Rotisserie also turns people into human beings and cuts across organizational barriers, linking people on a new and different plane.

John B.: One of the greatest before-and-after stories of my business life came when I got into the same league with a staff department manager whose help was vital to the success of my sales function. For years, we had trouble getting timely support. But as soon as I was able to walk into his office and ask about Eric Davis' latest injury, we suddenly found that every request for my department was being processed promptly, while others waited in line.

The best way to merge personal and business time in the workplace is to get your boss into your league. He will quickly understand and appreciate what you are doing, and will provide a buffer against others who scrutinize your time too closely. There is only one drawback: your boss may want Griffey Junior one day and make you an offer you can't refuse! The opposite of boss involvement is a big no-no: NEVER use a subordinate to do league work on company time. You would be asking someone to help you steal from the company and leaving them with written evidence of the crime.

YOUR LEAGUE AND YOUR TEAM

No matter how seriously you compete, there will always be some playful aspect to your activity. The roster is your own creation, and like any painting or piece of writing, it has the personal seal of the individual who created it.

The fun starts with naming your league and your team. For league names, places (including especially restaurants) are always popular, and they are certainly in the true Rotisserie spirit. The Georgetown Saloon, Shoreline Cafe, Donovan's, the Nassau Inn, and Phillips' Crab House are natural appellations. On the other hand, if you sneak into your corporate Board Room on Sunday and plug in a six-hour conference call to Florida and Arizona (for the latest spring training intelligence) you might want to pick a name that obscures what you were doing.

Some leagues include allusions to their purpose and reason for being. The Good Sports and Fair Play League was an offshoot formed by a group that had grown tired of an overbearing commissioner in their old league; the new league started with a rule banning commissioners. The Say Know to Drugs League, Dash for the Cash League, and All Charity League tell you something about the motivations of their members.

Other names are simply witty. Ten Men Out, Let's Play Too, and Freedom Alliance Rotisserie Teams (F.A.R.T) are names telling you that the participants have a sense of humor, or at least wish they did. Many leagues are named after long-gone baseball players, especially the colorful personalities with unusual names. Choo Choo Coleman, Rabbit Maranville, Marv Throneberry, Manny Mota and Billy Grabarkewitz all have leagues named after them.

OUR LEAGUE NAME

The best name game is fully under your personal control: naming your own team. The official Rotisserie method is to use your own name as if it were a city, and add something afterward to complete the team name. For example, John has long used the team name "Benson Burners," as if there was a place called Benson and they had a team there, called the Burners. The second part of the name is supposed to make a pun or witticism, in this case an allusion to the Bunsen Burner and use of the term Burner to describe a speedy player who steals 50 bases per year (John does like stolen bases, as you will hear at length later).

Most leagues are very liberal about how you name a team, and some leagues have no guidelines whatsoever. The oldest league in which we play has a tradition of getting the owner's first or last name into the team name somewhere. Pete DeCoursey's team is Rotten To DeCourseys. Bill Cunningham calls his team the Medical Bills, because he had great success with injury rehab cases like Pedro Guerrero and Andre Dawson in 1987. Bill Gray's team is cleverly called the Gray Matter, because he is a smart player. Randy's team is Bear 'n Grin It, a play on his last name, Baron. If you have the owner's name somewhere in the team name, you can call any team by the owner's name: the Bensons, the Bills, the Grays, etc., which often comes in handy if you are in a hurry.

Your league really should have some sort of theme for team names. After all, coming up with a creative team name is part of the fun!

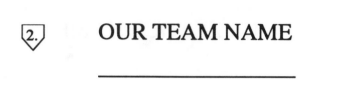

2. OUR TEAM NAME

People who get really excited about running their own baseball team may advance into accessory fun like team logos, team stationery, team T-shirts, and even team newsletters which berate the competition and provide regulation through ridicule for those who get out of line. These ideas may sound corny (schmaltzy if you're a New Yorker), but if you haven't tried it, don't knock it. At the worst, these amusements are a harmless waste of time; at best, they keep your mind off the subjects of unpaid bills and other personal hassles certainly a worthy purpose.

Randy B: My National League team, Smotantos, occupies a special place in my heart. This is partly because it has a proud tradition of success and partly because it is named after the beloved cocker spaniel from my college days, Smotanto. You can even add an appropriate slogan to your logo if you have the time to pursue such a crucial activity. Who knows, you may even intimidate other owners with your well thought out name and classy logo. (See page 43.)

2ND INNING

RULES PART I:
NAMES & NUMBERS

"Lou Piniella has three rules for us: be on time; play heads up; and ... I forget the third."
— *Todd Benzinger (who lost his job as Reds first baseman)*

THE LINEUP

- What positions should you use for each 23-man roster?
- What are the standard 8 catagories?
- Should your league use other catagories?
- How do you keep score?

Without rules, there wouldn't be any Rotisserie leagues. It was the elegant set of rules that first lifted Rotisserie baseball above the level of bar-room argument and into the formal arena of international cerebral rivalry.

In this chapter, we will review the key rules that need to be addressed in your league. Where there are choices to be made, or alternatives worth considering, we give you some pros and cons of the various possibilities.

ROSTERS

The most basic player-selection games are built around a simple lineup for each team: one catcher, one first baseman, etc. If you want the shortest possible selection process and the easiest stat-keeping, the "one of each" method is worth considering.

*We recommend the standard 23-man roster and
using players from either the American League
or the National League, not both.*

Throw in two starting pitchers (one righty and one lefty, if you want to be fancy) and one relief pitcher, and you can actually get a fantasy league started. Just be aware: every owner in your league is going to have a superstar at every position, and the winner will be determined mainly by luck and/or finding loopholes.

The standard Rotisserie format goes beyond the basic lineup to simulate a real major league roster, with reserves, platooners, and a full pitching staff with a realistic starting rotation and a complete bullpen.

The total number is 23 players per team:

- two catchers
- one first baseman
- one second baseman
- one third baseman
- one shortstop
- one middle infield (MI) backup, a 2B or SS
- one corner infield (CI) backup, a 1B or 3B
- five outfielders
- one extra hitter (any position or DH)
- nine pitchers

The standard 23-man roster is designed to go with ONE major league, American OR National. Using either league's population of players, there ideally should be twelve Rotisserie rosters.* You can have another number of teams in your league, but you will then have too few quality players (with more teams) or too many quality players (with less teams).

Before you decide what to do about roster sizes, you should consider that **the 23-man roster, using the 12 team format, is a carefully conceived method reflecting thoughtful design and flashes of brilliant insight. The result is a "balance of scarcity" with just the right number of players available to fill each position on each team.** When a Rotisserie league is formed and rosters completed, you want the pool of talent to accommodate each position, so that you just begin to run out of talent at each position when you finish filling out your rosters. You don't want too many good players left out of your league just because your roster requirements are too light at one position. Also, you don't want to make the requirements so high that there aren't enough players to fill every required position.

The 23-man roster is just about perfect for balancing the talent requirements at each position. It is so precise that some people can't even see how the roster rules affect the value of players. The differences are small, but they are real. You can see how the roster requirements affect what players are worth in your league, by thinking about the impact of different rules. If you required only three outfielders, instead of five, many good outfielders would be useless in your league. If you required four middle infielders instead of three, you would have to draft everyone who could possibly qualify at SS or 2B, even if they spent all their time on the bench. You want to keep these discrepancies to a minimum.

Depending on how tough you want to make your game, there are all kinds of possibilities for roster size and position requirements. The biggest decision is whether you want a "mixed

*In 1992, before expansion, the ideal NL League should have had 10 teams; existing leagues have had to decide the best way to add new teams.

league," drawing players from both AL and NL teams. Official Rotisserie rules say you should choose from the American League OR the National League, not both. **Many so-called Rotisserie leagues build twelve teams using players from the entire major league population.** The obvious result is a star at every position. During the 1990 World Series, the TV coverage included a comment that Oakland's lineup looked like a Rotisserie team. In a real Rotisserie league, you would rarely see such an awesome batting order. In a fantasy league mixing AL and NL players, you see murderous lineups all the time.

In choosing nine pitchers (or whatever number is selected) some leagues try to force a fixed number of starters and relievers. My advice is, don't make rules to differentiate. Far too many pitchers are moved in and out of the starting rotation, and sent to and from the bullpen. If you try to categorize pitchers, you will spend too much time worrying about your definitions, and not enough time enjoying the game. There may be valid reasons why you don't want rosters with all relievers or all starters, but there are better ways to deal with the possible problems, as explained in the pitching statistics section.

With 28 major league teams, there are 28 regular starting players at every position (for example, 28 first basemen and 28 third basemen). If you require ten teams to complete the 23-man roster outlined above, that means you will need only 30 corner infielders (in total, ten 1B's, ten 3B's, and ten either 1B or 3B). Obviously, with 56 major league regulars available to fill those 30 slots, you will be choosing your players from the cream of the crop.

You must decide for yourself what roster size is going to give you the most enjoyment, but I can give you a quick way to gauge the level of difficulty implicit in your roster requirements. I call it the "roster ratio." You simply count how many players are required to fill your league rosters in total, and how many players are available on the major league rosters from which you may choose, and calculate the ratio.

For example, if you have 12 teams choosing 23 players each

from the American or National League, then you need 276 players (12 x 23), and there are 350 players available (25 x 14 teams), for a ratio of 79% (276/350). If you fill out 12 rosters of 23 players each, using 28 major league teams, the ratio is only 39% [(23 x 12) / (25 x 28)]. Obviously, it is much easier to pick your teams when you can ignore half of the major league player population.

If your league has a "roster ratio" of 70% or higher, you have a fairly high level of difficulty, requiring a good knowledge of major league players. If your ratio is down around 50%, you are at the easy end of the spectrum.

We would advise every league to adopt the standard 23-man roster, with players from only the American League or the National League, unless you have a good reason to do something different. In addition to the previously-mentioned benefits of having balanced player scarcity at each position already thought out for you and having a competitive game that encourages everyone to know their major leaguers, here are two additional reasons in favor of the standard Rotisserie format:

• If you have smaller rosters (or use both AL and NL players to complete your teams) you will find that many good players are still available after you finish filling your rosters. A large pool of available talent causes problems. With plenty of good players available at any time during the season, one of the primary reasons for trading (needing a player) will be removed. A league without trades is usually boring. Also, having good players in the available pool can often create the unnatural situation where owners wish for their players to be hurt or disabled, so they can have access to the free agent pool to pick a replacement.

• Using the standard 23-man roster, with 12 NL or AL teams, will allow you to compare notes with people in other leagues. You will also get more benefit from the numerous books and periodicals about player values and recommended picks, if you follow the standard rules. When you tinker with roster size, funny things can happen to player values. Some players who have good value in a standard league will have no value in a league that uses fewer players, which is very confusing to the beginner.

If you are just beginning and want a simpler selection process, you can make the game easier by having fewer teams in your league. For example, you could start an American League Rotisserie with eight teams instead of twelve. You will find it fairly easy to fill out the eight rosters. Then as your league gains experience, you can increase the number of teams and automatically increase the level of difficulty, moving gradually, year by year, if that's what your league wants.

RESERVE LISTS AND FARM SYSTEMS

One of the popular methods to increase the required number of selected players, without putting a huge burden on every league member to know every player in baseball, **is the reserve list or supplemental roster.** Every owner selects a number of players in addition to the basic roster requirements. In most leagues, there are no position requirements for the reserve list; you can fill your reserve slots with all pitchers, or outfielders, or whatever you like.

Most leagues use the reserve or supplemental list to provide backup talent that can be called up when other players are hurt, demoted, or simply inactive. The depth consideration is especially attractive as a method to reward those owners who do their homework most thoroughly.

Another use of a supplemental list is the long-term storage of minor league talent. Many leagues have a minor league draft after they finish filling out their rosters with major league players. The minor leaguers can be activated by their owners after the players become active, or the farmhands can be carried over to future years if they don't make it to major leagues quickly.

The official Rotisserie rules provide for both a Reserve List and a Farm System. The reserve list is a repository for

major league players who have been disabled, waived, or sent back to the minors. Their Rotisserie owners continue to hold their reserve players within their franchise, while they are also allowed to pick replacements for their active rosters. When a disabled player returns, the owner then must decide whether to keep the replacement, or to reactivate the original player and release the replacement.

The Rotisserie Farm System is filled through a minor league draft, held immediately after the major league rosters have been filled. The official rules call for a two-round draft each year, with a maximum of three players in the farm system at any one time (including carry-overs from the previous season). There is, however, nothing especially harmful about allowing a longer draft (say five rounds each year) and/or a larger farm system (say ten or fifteen players per franchise), except the possibility that one owner who does the most intense study of minor leaguers could leave his opponents in the dust. Whatever the size and method of selecting farm system players, the usual rule is to require that players may be activated as soon as they get promoted to the major leagues, and must be activated or let go after they lose their rookie status.

One of the most popular forms of Rotisserie baseball, named Ultra by its creators (the same geniuses who created original Rotisserie), uses a 40-man roster for each team, with 23 players active and 17 players on reserve at anytime. The Ultra game is described in Volume II of this series; it uses a fairly complicated format and is intended for people who have reached the advanced stages of Rotisserie mania. The basic notion of a 40-man roster, however, is an idea that can appeal to beginners as well.

If you decide to start a mixed league (AL and NL players both included), the 40-man roster is an excellent way to reduce the available player pool and eliminate most of the problems associated with a too-large pool of available players as mentioned above. A 12-team league, using 40 players per team, would take 480 players in the draft. One standard NL Rotisserie league and one standard AL league would take 552 players, so there really isn't any big difference in the number and quality of players left when you get done.

3. The positions for our league are:

A)	☐ 2 Catchers*	☐	Other _____
B)	☐ 1 1B*	☐	Other_____
C)	☐ 1 2B*	☐	Other_____
D)	☐ 1 3B*	☐	Other_____
E)	☐ 1 SS*	☐	Other_____
F)	☐ 1 Middle Inf (2B or SS)*	☐	Other_____
G)	☐ 1 Corner Inf (1B or 3B)*	☐	Other_____
H)	☐ 5 OF*	☐	Other_____
I)	☐ 1 Extra Hitter (any position)*	☐	Other_____
J)	☐ 9 Pitchers*	☐	Other_____

4. The total number of active players per team (add the positions above) is:

☐ 23*
☐ Other_____

5. The pitchers may be

☐ any number of starters and relievers*
☐ Other_____

We have indicated our recommended choices for rules throughout the book by *.

6. The number of teams in our league is:

☐ 8
☐ 9
☐ 10
☐ 11
☐ 12*
☐ Other_____

7. Players are used from:

☐ *NL only
☐ *AL only
☐ Both Leagues

8. Will the league have a Reserve List? (See page 29 for a further discussion.) ☐ Yes* ☐ No

If yes, how many players on the RL?_____

If yes, when will the players be chosen?_____

9. Will the league have a Farm System?

☐ Yes ☐ No

If yes, how many players in the FS?_____

If yes, when will the players be chosen?_____

> *Baseball statistics are like a girl in a bikini; they show you a lot, but not everything."* — *Toby Harrah*

Our first word on statistics is that you should always consider the single activity that will absorb much of your time after you get into this Rotisserie game: you will be reading box scores. Whatever your favorite stat category may be, don't use Rotisserie baseball as a way to force other people to look at it. If it isn't in the daily box score, it shouldn't be in your league statistics.

The standard for statistics is the original Rotisserie League. They use eight categories, four for batters and four for pitchers. The batters are measured in batting average (BA), home runs (HR), runs batted in (RBI), and stolen bases (SB). Pitchers are rated in earned run average (ERA), wins (W), saves (SV), and baserunners per inning (BPI) ratio. To get a BPI ratio (often called just "ratio") you simply add hits plus walks and divide by innings pitched. You don't count batters hit-by-pitch or safe on an error, etc., because these events are not printed in the basic box score and reading the box score is your daily passion once you start playing. These are the "eight basic categories."

THE 8 BASIC ROTISSERIE CATAGORIES

BATTERS	PITCHERS
• AVERAGE	• ERA
• HOME RUNS	• WINS
• RBI	• SAVES
• STOLEN BASES	• RATIO

One of the most popular deviations from standard Rotisserie rules is the alteration of stat categories. You can understand why the stats could become a point of contention in many leagues: the foundation of the game is a contest to see who can pick the "best" team, and a big part of this argument is the definition of what "best" means.

Many leagues add runs scored (R) to the hitters' measures, and innings pitched (IP) or strikeouts (SO) to the pitchers' statistics. We can understand and support the reasons for these categories, and they are stats that can be found easily in every box score. Also, as you will see in the KEEPING SCORE section below, it isn't complex or difficult to add another category or two. At the worst, if you add categories, you might end up spending a little more time in perusing your standings, or spending a little more money if you employ a professional stat service.

As in the case of roster size, there is one good reason to stick with the eight basic categories: many books and publications give advice and player rankings and values assuming you are using these eight categories. If you change stats, you will find that many of these aids don't apply to your league without some fine-tuning or careful interpretation.

After that word of caution, we encourage more experienced and serious Rotisserians to experiment a little with stat categories. The original Rotisserie League and the rule-making Rotisserie League Baseball Association have made some small but innovative changes over the years, usually in reaction to real-world experiences. Although they haven't moved an inch on the subject of the eight stat categories, there have been some minor footnote-type changes and there is no reason to believe that the eight categories are listed on stone tablets (sacred tablets, yes, but stone, no).

The subject of statistics is a common ground where Rotisserie leaguers meet sabermetricians, the people who study baseball facts and figures. If you have an interest in both subjects — the contest to see who can pick the best team and the ongoing accumulation of pure knowledge about baseball — you will double your fun. If you aren't the sabermetric type (and if you haven't heard of sabermetrics before picking up this book, you are probably not the type) my advice is to leave sabermetrics to

34

the sabermetricians. In other words, if somebody tells you that Rotisserie baseball doesn't include accurate measures of a baseball player's true value, just smile and say, "Yes, I know. But it's a great deal of fun, anyway."

Sabermetric statisticians may say that would have more fun if you changed your game to include more sophisticated measures such as runs created, total offensive average and quality starts, but most of the people who say such things are not experts on fun, they are only experts on sophisticated measures. Indeed, some of the least enjoyable fantasy baseball rules have been invented by some of the people who know the most about how to measure a player's performance.

Rotisserie leagues are a model of baseball roster management, just as chess is a model of ancient warfare. The point of this analogy is that you could make numerous changes in the game of chess to make it more like real warfare, but these changes would not likely improve the enjoyment of the people who play chess; indeed, any "improvements" could turn out to be quite a nuisance. When you manage a Rotisserie team, you are concerned mainly with the management aspect — the juggling of the roster to deal with injuries and changing roles. The statistical aspect of Rotisserie baseball is just a by-product.

One of the most common misunderstandings among people who don't play Rotisserie is that the people who do play are all statistical nuts. Much too often, you hear a television broadcaster or baseball beat writer talk about home/road, grass/turf, day/night breakdowns in a denigrating manner and blame the proliferation of such statistics on "those Rotisserie people who want every possible statistic."

Rotisserie people like simplicity in their numbers. Look at the stats that Rotisserie leagues use for hitters: BA, HR and RBI are the "big three" numbers, the ones that you always used to see on the backs of baseball cards way back in the 1950's. These are the stats most commonly used on TV graphics when a hitter comes to the plate. To these three numbers, Rotisserie leagues add only stolen bases, an important measure of speed that is not at all reflected in the big three stats for an offensive player.

Even if you choose to experiment, we recommend keeping your stats simple. The golden rule: if it isn't in the box score, don't use it. Yes, we know, batting average isn't in the traditional box score, but hits and at bats are two of the four hitting numbers that are always displayed. And if you can't see the link between batting average and figures like 0 for 5, or 3 for 4, then you shouldn't be reading this book, anyway.

Before leaving the subject of stats, **we will dwell on a couple of the best variations and list some of the other possibilities with their pros and cons.**

First, we are all in favor of runs scored. Since the whole purpose of baseball is to score runs, we really can't see any reason to leave them out. They are one of the four columns in the most basic box score. HR and RBI both emphasize the value of middle-of-the-order hitters, while diminishing the importance of leadoff and number two hitters. Stolen bases will raise the value of a leadoff hitter, but the main purpose of the leadoff man is to score runs, not to steal bases. One more consideration is that runs, over the course of a season, will reflect most of the good things that an offensive player can do on the field: getting a walk or an extra base hit, going from first to third on a single, advancing a base on a groundout, tagging up on a sacrifice fly, etc.

The other category that we would add to the the basic eight would be innings pitched. Many leagues already have IP rules, stated in terms of minimums that must be reached to avoid incurring some penalty. The main reason for these minimum IP rules is that middle relievers with low ERA's and low ratios are disproportionately easy to obtain in Rotisserie drafts and auctions; it is too easy to do well with a pitching staff comprised of Roger Clemens and eight relief pitchers. Another problem is that teams with a big lead in August may be tempted to cut down their number of active pitchers and thus reduce the risk of losing precious points in ERA and ratio; rosters with "ghost" pitchers may be clever gamesmanship, but they are no fun for the opposition to watch.

Rather than set a minimum IP requirement with some complicated method of imposing penalties*, why not just make innings pitched a category? If your gut reaction is that IP are just a measure of time spent on the field (like at bats for hitters) consider that an inning pitched is an accomplishment. Any fool can walk up to the plate and get some at bats, but it takes a genuine major league pitcher to get three outs from the opposition. When a pitcher completes an inning, he is doing a valuable service for his team. True, some innings are better than others, but every victory requires nine innings from the pitching staff.

Some other categories that you might want to consider ...

• On Base Percentage (OBP): The main virtue of OBP is that it includes walks. And if you owned Jack Clark during the years when he hit around .240 while carrying one of the highest OBP's in baseball, you probably favor OBP over BA already. Many newspaper box scores are beginning to show walks and plate appearances, in addition to hits and at bats, and papers like USA TODAY give you OBP in the weekly stats page, so it isn't too far-fetched.

• Net stolen bases: Many realists want to impose a penalty

---

*Sports Forum Fantasy Baseball on CompuServe developed one of the most interesting and most punitive methods for dealing with all-reliever pitching rosters. In 1991, they raised their minimum IP requirement to 1170 innings per year (many leagues use only 900 or 1000). The interesting part is not the minimum, but the penalty and its origin. With a philosophy of "make the punishment fit the crime," the intent of the penalty is to fill in any shortfall of innings with the worst possible pitcher. And who would the worst possible pitcher be? Why Curt Wardle, of course! No, Wardle is not the worst pitcher in baseball history. In fact, in 1985 he was good enough to get into 50 games for the Indians and Twins, winning eight of them. Wardle didn't pitch very well, however. He finished the year with a 6.18 ERA and a ratio of 1.64. The penalty is an addition of "bad innings" to get you up to the 1170 IP minimum, using Wardle's stats (rounded): a 6.00 ERA and a 1.667 ratio. The originators of this rule, who later presented it to Compuserve, were simply looking for a pitcher who pitched a lot, but didn't really belong in the major leagues. In 1985, that man was Curt Wardle.

on baserunners who just run and run until they get thrown out, usually hurting their team. The logical argument is that if a runner gets caught attempting to steal second base, he doesn't just lose second base, he also wastes the value of the runner at first base. Some people would define net steals as stolen bases minus times caught stealing (SB — CS). Harsher evaluators recommend subtracting double the number of times caught stealing (SB—2 x CS).

• Strikeouts by pitchers: If you don't adopt IP as a measure of pitcher volume, strikeouts is another good category that will encourage every owner to use a good number of starting pitchers.

• Pitchers' win/loss percentage: Another device to steer roster-builders toward starting pitchers and away from ace relievers and setup men, W/L percentage has the unpleasant side effect of placing a huge value on starting pitchers with good luck. If you like random numbers and wild cards, this is a fun statistic, but if you want numbers that reflect a player's true performance, this isn't one of them. The same thing can be said of any stats that include losses in addition to wins (wins minus losses, losses as a separate category, etc.)

• Errors: One aspect of baseball that doesn't get into the standard eight categories is defense. The best argument we have heard (and it's still a bit feeble) is that stolen bases reflect speed, and speed means good defense. Obviously, you can get errors by looking in any box score, and the people who designed baseball scoreboards must have had a high opinion of the importance of errors, because they put them right up there alongside runs and hits. Errors are better than nothing (we think), but if you use them, you will have to expand and tighten your position eligibility rules. Everyone will want players who qualify at middle infield (the source of most errors) but play mostly outfield. In 1986 we played in a league where Roy Smalley was among the most valuable players in the game, because we counted errors, and Smalley was a DH who qualified at SS and hit 20 homers. My advice is to be very careful about position requirements if you decide to use errors, and if you're not sure, don't do it.

• Fielding percentage: Another attempt to get defense into the game, we don't like the percentage method. Fielding chances are not easily obtainable on a daily basis. Also, there are some positions (such as 1B) that produce many chances and very few errors. Our advice is to wait until we have better measures of defense, such as Pete DeCoursey's defensive average, more readily available in the daily media.

Just about any stat that appears in a newspaper, magazine or book can be used for Rotisserie purposes. Our last word on this subject amplifies the first: don't let the stat tables tell you how to play. You don't have to use every available category. There is nothing wrong with the basic eight. More people have gotten more pleasure (and pain) from those eight categories than from any other statistics in the history of the game.

10. Our league will have

- ☐ 8* catagories.
- ☐ 9
- ☐ 10
- ☐ Other_____

Catagories

11. Standard:

- ☐ BA
- ☐ HR
- ☐ RBI
- ☐ SB

- ☐ W
- ☐ S
- ☐ ERA
- ☐ BPI

- ☐ R
- ☐ IP
- ☐ OBP
- ☐ NSB
- ☐ K

- ☐ WL%
- ☐ E
- ☐ F%
- ☐ Other _____

12. Is there a minimum number of IP per team?

Yes ☐   No ☐

If yes, what is the penalty if the team does not meet the requirements?_____

_____

KEEPING SCORE

The scoring method of Rotisserie baseball is one of the elegant simplicities that makes the game so enjoyable. Every participant is presented with a multi-front struggle and a different group of rivals on every front. Nothing could be better to stimulate and maintain interest in the great puzzle of roster management.

STANDARD SCORING

Teams are ranked from top to bottom in each stat category. Every team gets one point in each category, plus one point for each team below them in each category. For example, the team with the most home runs in a ten-team league gets ten points; the second best gets nine points, etc., and the lowest team in HR gets one point. In a twelve-team league, topping a category is worth twelve points. The total number of available points is always equal to the number of teams times the number of categories. The highest possible score with ten teams and eight categories would be 80 points. With twelve teams and ten categories, there are 120 possible points. The team with the most points at year-end wins the league.

Much of the complex strategy (and fun) in Rotisserie comes from analyzing and juggling the stat categories during the season. There are natural trade-offs that require attention. Most of the hitters who produce homers and RBI are weak in the stolen bases category. The pitchers who get the most wins, the starters, never get any saves. Soon after you start playing, you learn to appreciate the value of "multi-category" hitters — those wonderful athletes who give you both home runs and stolen bases, such as Barry Bonds and Jose Canseco. Some of them give you the value of two players combined.

We have an entire chapter about managing your roster and watching the categories. To get started, you just have to be aware of the method. The highlight of usual Rotisserie scoring is that it pits you against specific opponents in each category: the teams immediately above you, and below you, in the standings. When you pass another team, you take a point away from them, while gaining a point yourself. When another team passes you, they gain a point which you lose.

The standard method of scoring means that the way you manage your roster will affect the point totals of other teams. Rotisserie fits the category of games like tennis, bridge, boxing and poker; when you do something beneficial, you prevent your opponents from scoring. There is "defense" in Rotisserie scoring. You can actually take points away from the opposition. For example, if you have a big lead in home runs, you can trade one of your sluggers to another team that will then pass your arch rival in the HR category. You lose nothing, but you take a point away from one team and give it to another.

Some fantasy leagues use one-dimensional scoring: you just accumulate points on your own roster, without affecting the other teams. There is nothing wrong with this method. Sports and games like bowling and golf work the same way: you go out and do the best you can, and when the game is over you compare your score to the opponents to see who won. Personally, we like the complexity of a game that requires you to watch your opponents and constantly react to them. If you have a limited amount of time, however, you might like the simpler method better; it takes less time to focus on one roster than to be constantly watching ten or twelve opponents and monitoring their strategies.

41

⌂ **13.** Our league will use the ☐ standard*
☐ one-dimensional method
of scoring.

Concerning stat-keeping, we recommend using a professional service. Most leagues get started with one owner volunteering to do the number-crunching, but this method usually creates problems. There is an inherent conflict of interest, obviously, but that isn't the main problem. Most of the leagues that use do-it-yourself scoring run into difficulties when the volunteer loses interest or takes a vacation during the summer. There is nothing more disconcerting than having your flow of numbers interrupted in the heat of a pennant race. It can also be very time-consuming, even if the volunteer overcomes the other drawbacks.

⌂ **14.** Who will keep our stats?

☐ Stat service*   Name _____
☐ Someone in league Name _____
☐ Non-owner   Name _____

We have a section recommending some professional stat services (see Chapter 10). The main point is that you should be concerned about a company's size and stability, not their prices. Many of the smaller outfits may start out with good intentions, but then run into problems caused by illness or financial difficulty or some other unforeseeable factor. Our advice is to ask for references, preferably some people who live near you, and check those references carefully. Sometimes, you can even make a new friend or find a new league by calling to check on a stat service.

Randy B.: It's a small world . . . Jerry Heath, who operates one of the leading stat services, lived next to me in my freshman dorm at the University of Florida. He contacted me a few years ago wondering if it was the same Randy Baron from 20 years earlier when he saw one of our annual Rotisserie books. Looking back, it's nice to know both of us probably had our priorities straight when we watched baseball instead of studying.

It is important to resolve any questions about the rules before the auction or draft so your league will function smoothly all year.

3RD INNING

RULES PART II:
THE DRAFT OR AUCTION:

FILLING YOUR ROSTER

"Prospects are a dime a dozen."
— *Charlie Finley*

THE LINEUP

When should you hold the draft or auction?

Which rules are most important to have your league's draft or auction go smoothly?

Who should be your auctioneer?

What are the advantages of having an auction rather than a draft?

Once your league has selected a roster size, position requirements, eligible player population, and method of keeping score, you can begin to pick your players. (**Never start choosing players until all these questions have been settled first.**) Most leagues have a "draft day" around the same time as major league baseball's opening day, but you can start and finish any time you want.

> ## ROTISSERIE RECOMMENDATION
> Try to have your auction or draft near opening day.

If your league can assemble as one group at one time, there is nothing more exciting and entertaining than a genuine Rotisserie draft or auction. The standard Rotisserie League draft date is the Saturday after opening day. **There are several good reasons why your league should stay as close as possible to the official Draft Day:**

(1) After major league teams have finalized their opening day rosters, **you can avoid picking players who fail in spring training** and go back to the minor leagues, or go to Japan, or retire. It's no fun starting the year with a roster full of players who are toiling at Richmond or Albuquerque or Yokahama; in fact it's downright embarrassing!

(2) **After a few major league games have been played, you can look in the box scores and see who is actually getting playing time on the field.** Having a bench player on your roster is a painful experience, especially if you counted on him to play every day. A non-playing major leaguer is usually worse than a prospect who gets sent down. Most leagues allow for replacement of minor league demotees but don't provide easy corrective steps for players who get benched. If you have the benefit of seeing the first few days box scores, you will at least postpone the disappointment of seeing your high-priced talent take a seat in the dugout while others make their pitches and swing their bats.

(3) If you have a fixed date on your calendar, with a strong point of reference such as Opening Day, **you will eliminate one of the toughest problems of league administration: scheduling.** If you organize a league in December with everyone understanding that draft day will be "around opening day," you will be dismayed in March to learn that your twelve owners have

twelve different ideas about when their draft should be held. Usually, given three weeks notice, there will be no date when more than five of them can attend. So just write it into your league rules now: "On the Saturday following opening day, at 12:00 noon," and there won't be too much bickering when the day approaches.

If the Saturday after opening day doesn't work for your league, move the date back, but not forward (well, maybe Friday night after opening day would be OK). You can have a draft day two or three weeks into the season, or even in May or June if there is no alternative. It is NEVER too late in the season to get started and have some fun. The ideal, however, is as soon as possible after the major league season has started rolling.

15. Our ☐ draft or ☐ auction will be held on_____.
It will be   ☐ at a meeting
               ☐ by phone.

If your league has unusual logistical problems such as people scattered around the country, you may have to conduct your draft by telephone, and you may want to start very early, even in mid winter. We play in one long-distance league that starts the draft in October (!) and moves slowly through several phases. The good players all disappear by December, other regulars get taken in March, and we get down to the scrubs and less important platooners right around the end of spring training when major league managers are focused on the same names and final selections as we are. It is an unusual method, but it works nicely.

As with all rules, you have some choices to make, even if you follow the official Rotisserie methods in every other aspect. **One of the biggest decisions that you have to make is whether to select your players with a simple draft or to use an auction.** In the "football style" draft method, owners take turns naming players and each player goes to the owner who names him. In an auction (as you would expect) each name goes up for bid and the highest bidder gets the player. To keep things sane, there is a predetermined spending limit or salary cap. And the "money" in the auction can be play money or just "points." You don't have to use real dollars. Most leagues do have a real prize fund, but it can be very small and it's not necessary. Some of the leagues that we have enjoyed most are run by Sports Forum on CompuServe (see chapter 10), and they have absolutely no money involved.

The auction is the essence of Rotisserie League Baseball. Everything you have ever heard about player valuation, pricing methods, long-term contracts, player dumping, the one dollar special, etc., all come from Rotisserie auction practices and terminology. Indeed, the auction and player valuation are so important in Rotisserie leagues that many people get too absorbed with the question of how much they should bid for each player and they forget about the other aspects of the game.

Some analytical types become so myopic about the auction that they spend the entire summer thinking about what they should have bid, and then after the final stats are in, they spend the autumn and winter calculating precisely what each player's price should have been in the previous year's auction. We will bash these backward-looking methods at length later, but the point is: don't let auction technicalities take your attention away from the question of which players are going to do better or worse in the coming season.

Although the auction method has a number of problems which result from the complexity, an auction can be more enjoyable for the following reasons:

1. **The auction introduces a game element that makes the Rotisserie league different from all other fantasy leagues.** With good skills and money management, you can overcome shortcomings in your knowledge of players.

2. **There are numerous books, guides and reference materials** (see chapter 10) that will help you in an auction if you have no experience.

3. **The auction creates more opportunities for excitement;** in a draft, the major thrill is getting a player before someone else.

4. **The auction introduces many psychological possibilities.** You can bluff by bidding on a player you do not really want, put pressure on an owner if you know he really likes a player or have a tense battle if there is scarcity in a category or at a particular position.

5. **You see people boxed into corners when they run out of money;** in a draft, filling up positions is the only way you have problems.

6. **The draft is a great equalizer** — you can have owners who know very little about players who can do well if they understand the auction concept. Conversely, owners with great baseball knowledge can have a disastrous auction.

Once the auction is over, forget about player prices immediately; they do not matter anymore until you get into late-season planning for next year.

The whole range of activity surrounding auctions is deeply absorbing. If you want real Rotisserie baseball — including the pleasure you get from telling someone that you got Cecil Fielder for $2 back in 1990 —then you have to follow the auction format. Most leagues use the auction and are glad they do.

WHY YOU MIGHT PREFER A DRAFT

There are some valid arguments against the auction method, however, and there are valid reasons why a simple draft might be better, especially if you are just a beginner.

The single strongest argument against the auction is not a condemnation; it is a simple fact: the auction becomes a game within itself. Very often the owner who wins a Rotisserie league is the owner who handles himself best during the auction. The auction tests a whole range of skills that are somewhat removed from the basic contest to see who can select the best baseball talent. Memory, concentration, intuition, reading body lan-

49

guage, budgeting, money management, keeping track of other people's finances and understanding price theory will all affect the performance of your team. You might prefer that these subjects not enter into the picture. Many Rotisserians love the intricate gamesmanship that comes with the auction (we are fascinated by these subjects ourselves!) but many baseball fans can live without them.

You need both baseball knowledge and auction skill (and numerous other skills) to win a Rotisserie league. In no way can a nerd with a computer come into a draft room and kick the butts of ten people who know much more about baseball than he does. But the auction can be a great equalizer. Many jocks, ex-jocks, and real baseball scouts and coaches will tell you it is a humbling experience to see an obvious non-athlete, non-scout assemble a superior roster in a Rotisserie auction. When two people have approximately equal knowledge and insight concerning baseball, the one with the better ability to manage money and read poker faces during the auction will usually do better in a Rotisserie league.

Some other points that might make you prefer a simple draft:

1. **An auction takes longer than a draft** (much longer if the participants are beginners).

2. **The draft method usually does a better job of separating the well-prepared drafters from the people who didn't do their homework.** In a draft, when a player's names comes up, he is instantly gone. In an auction, when a player comes up for bid, anyone can stop and think: "Oh, yeah, I forgot about him. He's good. I bid $10!"

3. **The draft requires less record-keeping.** During an auction, everyone has to keep track of player salaries, how much money has been spent and how much each owner has left relative to his spending limit, if they want to compete at a serious level. After an auction there are salary records that need to be maintained, along with contract status to determine what the player's

salary should be in future years.

4. **Finally, there is no shortage of excitement in a simple draft.** The "sudden death" nature of players disappearing, as soon as they are named, creates continuous tension and excitement. For those of you who choose not to follow the auction path, we have plenty of advice on strategy and tactics for the complexities that can arise during a "simple" draft.

One central, philosophical question in the draft-or-auction argument is which method is "most like real baseball." The pro-auction people, for example, will make fun of the simple draft as "like football" and therefore undesirable. That argument is cogent, but it is gradually losing strength as baseball's annual draft and Rotisserie's own minor league draft become bigger parts of the game with each passing year. If real baseball executives have to deal with first rounds, "sandwich picks" and related terminolgy, why shouldn't Rotisserians be involved in such matters?

Your choice may come down to the question of whether you want to simulate the role of the Scouting Director, or the General Manager. To test your ability to evaluate talent and see the future of player performance, the simple draft is a fine process. If you want to face the problems that have kept Lou Gorman and Fred Claire awake at night, trying to assemble the most talent within a fixed budget, that is the essence of the auction.

BASIC DRAFT RULES

To begin any draft, find some impartial method to determine a draft order. You can draw lots, pick numbers from a hat, cut cards or whatever you want. If you have people in faraway places, you may need to be creative. One league uses the last digit of the Dow Jones industrial average as a random number generator; each of the ten owners gets a digit from 0 through 9 and they start watching on January 2 each year. The only problem is that the same digits can come up repeatedly,

51

delaying the process for days and even weeks, so you have to allow plenty of time if you choose some esoteric method outside of your personal control.

Don't worry excessively about draft order. During the late 1980's, American League drafts gave a definite advantage (Rickey Henderson) to the owner who got first pick, but except for that the process has not been lopsided toward either end. You should reverse the draft order after each round, so in a ten team league the owner who gets the first pick doesn't pick again until the 20th and 21st, then the 40th and 41st, etc. The owner with the 10th pick also gets the 11th, so the "loser" in the draft order lottery ends up getting two of the top 11 players, which isn't a bad deal.

As simple as the round-by-round draft should be, there are innumerable ways to mess it up. People will draft players out of turn and claim players who are not in the available pool (minor leaguers for example). They will put players at positions where they are not eligible, name players who have been taken already and disappear when it's their turn to pick.

The simplest rule to deal with such problems and to prevent their occurrence in the future is to be uniformly harsh. We suggest a rule such as: "Any draft pick which is delayed, out of turn, involves an unavailable player or an ineligible position or is otherwise improper will be null and void and will be recorded as a "pass" as soon as the error is noted. The person making such an illegal pick will be allowed a make-up selection after the entire draft is finished."

You may be tempted, in a spirit of good sportsmanship, to let the erring party make a replacement pick at the earliest possible moment after the mistake is discovered, but you will likely do more harm than good with such a policy. Some selfish individuals will see a reason to keep their mouths shut when they know that an error has been committed, because they want to postpone the corrected pick until after all the good players are gone. Trying to figure out how to fit make-up picks into the middle of a draft will open the door to confusion and argument. When people realize that there is no mercy, they will pay closer attention and make fewer mistakes.

If it seems too harsh to nullify a second round pick and replace it with a 24th round pick after the draft is over, you could try a rule providing for a makeup round in the middle of the draft. For example, any make-up picks due to errors that have been detected in the first ten rounds will be corrected in a special makeup round between the tenth and eleventh rounds. But then you still have the risk that a second round error will not be discovered until near the end of the draft (and that competitors who see the error will not want to tell anyone). So we come back to the same advice: don't mix in mercy if it's going to interfere with clarity and simplicity.

Finally, **you need a time limit appropriate to the circumstances of your draft.** If everyone is gathered in one room and is half-way prepared, three minutes is plenty of time to make every selection. (Don't forget to allow for the people in the first and last positions, when they have to make two picks at a time.) Most people should be able to choose their player within a few seconds or a minute at most; many will go very quickly through the entire draft. Five minutes would be too generous; ten minutes is crazy. A draft with 276 picks (a standard 12-team league) could take 46 hours if you allow ten minutes per pick, so we hope you get the point.

In the long-distance telephone draft that we mentioned above starting in October, that league allowed up to one full day for each person to agonize over their picks. Most people didn't take anywhere near a full day, but a few were determined to prove the axiom that any job will expand to fill its budgets for time and money. And there are always people who want to stretch every rule, no matter how generous. We had one owner who would always find a way for his pick to come around on a Friday and then he would disappear for a long weekend to consider his alternatives. He isn't in the league any more.

Whatever rule you select for speed of selection, keep it simple (no exceptions or variations) and make the punishment for transgression swift and sure. It doesn't hurt to beef up any rule with a provision that habitual offenders will be tossed out of your league unceremoniously, with the league taking a lien on their house for compensation.

THE ROTISSERIE AUCTION

When it comes to the rules for the standard Official Rotisserie Auction there is really no substitute for the source authority, the Waggoner/Sklar Rotisserie League Baseball book. If you intend to follow the Rotisserie recipe exactly, you should get their book every year and study it religiously. There is nothing like getting information direct from the source.

ROTISSERIE RECOMMENDATION
Use a fraction or multiple of $260 for the amount
each owner has to spend.

The Rotisserie method allows each owner to spend $260 to fill out his 23-man roster. You can use $26, $2.60, or 260 toothpicks, but if you stick to some fraction or multiple of $260, you will be able to make sense out of all the annual advice guides that tell you how much each player is supposed to be worth and you will be able to compare your prices with people in other leagues. The auction starts with somebody naming a player and bidding $1 or more.

The bids increase in increments of $1 or more. (Don't allow bids of 50 cents or $1.01 or $1.10, etc., unless you want your auction to take all summer.) Bidding moves in order around the room to the left or right (in most leagues, it is not a free-for-all) and keeps going until everyone has dropped out except one bidder, who gets the player in question at the last price bid. This price then becomes the player's "salary" for the coming year.

If you are in a league with a smart, strong auctioneer and a friendly group, it is not necessary to make everyone bid in order when it is their turn. You can speed things up by letting people just bid when they want a player.

Obviously, impossible bids are not allowed. No one can bid more money than he has left and no one can bid on a player who cannot fit onto their roster. So, for example, an owner who has already purchased nine pitchers (the full quota) cannot then bid on a tenth pitcher just because he likes the sound of the guy's name. Each owner's spending limit is actually his total money, minus $1 for each unfilled slot after the one being bid upon. For example, in the very beginning with $260 and 23 open slots, every owner must preserve $22 for the remaining positions on his roster, so the highest possible bid is $238 [260 - (22 x 1)]. When someone has $32 left and ten slots remaining open, they cannot bid more than $23 [32 — (9x1)].

ROTISSERIE RECOMMENDATION
Allow plenty of time for your auction.

If the auction sounds like a long and complicated process, that's because it is. **For the first auction of a new league, you should allow all day, literally eight to ten hours, to complete the whole process.** From the time everyone starts getting settled, through the miscellaneous recaps and questions and arguments and restroom breaks, up until the last player is taken and the last dollar accounted for, ten hours can be absorbed easily.

You will hear people say, "Oh, my Rotisserie auction went smoothly and took only two and a half hours." Chances are, the person telling this story is someone who plays in a league of well-prepared veterans who had their rosters half completed with players carried over from the previous years, with an expert auctioneer running the show, and nobody ever lost track or wanted to use a toilet or had to make a phone call. And the person is probably exaggerating anyway. It is much better to allow eight hours or more and get finished in only six, than to advertise the auction as a six hour affair and have everyone getting home two or three hours late for dinner. There is going to be enough friction with spouses during the six-month long season; don't get started on the wrong foot.

Four valuable suggestions to help your auction run smoothly:

(1) **When it's someone's turn to nominate a player for bid, you cannot allow them to pass.** Everyone, when the time comes, must name a player and bid $1 or more. Like most rules, the importance of this little item isn't visible until you see a league trying to play without it. We saw such a case involving this rule. Two owners bought a bunch of high-priced players early in the auction. One ended up needing ten players and having only $10 left to spend; he was locked into $1 bids for the duration. The other fellow also needed ten more players, and he had $11, meaning he could pay $2 for one player and then $1 each for all the rest. Neither one of them wanted to name a player after that point, because they didn't want to have someone else bid $2 and shut them out.

So they just kept saying "pass" every time it was their turn to name a player. Finally, there were only the two of them left in the auction. The one with $11 finally named a player and bought him for $1, because the other guy couldn't raise to $2.

The guy with exactly $10 and ten vacant slots then refused to name a player. "Pass," he said.

"I pass, too," said the other. "Now you must name someone."

"But whoever I name for one dollar, you will bid $2. It isn't fair." This fiasco could have gone on forever, but the other people in the room started hooting and hollering and throwing small objects until they started naming players.

So make sure your league forbids passing when it's time to nominate a player and write it into the rules clearly.

(2) **Always try to find an auctioneer who is not an owner**

in your league. If you are starting a new league and have a number of novices, don't even think about the possibility of letting one of your league's novice owners function as auctioneer. It's hard enough to keep track of your own roster and spending limits. If someone tells you they can be auctioneer and owner at the same time, let them prove it with somebody else's league. You need an independent auctioneer who has no other duties during your draft.

The best way to get a volunteer for this thankless job is to send one of your owners to be auctioneer for another league and take one of the other league's owners to be auctioneer for your draft day. Volunteers will be easier to find than you might imagine. Some of the more astute and more competitive Rotisserians know that you can learn a lot about the market, see which players are commanding high prices and which are being overlooked by running an auction for another league.

When selecting an auctioneer, be very concerned about capability and honesty, and not at all concerned about warmth of personality. An abrasive autocrat with sharp accounting skills makes a good auctioneer, while a bumbling, well-intentioned good neighbor who tries to please everybody is destined to make everyone suffer, himself included.

(3) **Decide on a schedule for a break (or two) before the auction starts.** At any point during any auction, some of the owners are going to feel like they are totally in control and others are going to feel hopelessly disoriented. And these roles can change. The guy who has everything in place after the tenth round, with visions of pennants dancing in his head, may suddenly come unglued in the twelfth round when he discovers his remaining bankroll is smaller than he thought it was. The point is, there is never going to be any moment when everyone wants to take a break. If you set your schedule before starting, no one is going to feel unfairly treated. Adopt a rule for breaks "after the tenth round" for example, not "at four o'clock." You don't want to stop in the middle of bidding on a player.

(4) Make frequent reviews of everyone's roster and money. The best method is a billboard size roster and spending summary in the front of your draft room, but such a visual aid is a huge amount of work, and possibility not worth the effort. Whatever help you decide to provide, such as reviewing money and number of roster slots remaining after the tenth, fifteenth, and twentieth rounds, somebody is going to squawk that it isn't fair to those who are keeping good records on their own, while it gives extra help to those who are having trouble keeping track. Don't listen to them. The people with excellent records are going to do well anyway. It is in the best interest of the league to keep the stragglers up to speed and avoid time-consuming mistakes and delays due to uncertainty.

Finally, what about computers in the draft room? Many of the problems discussed above would simply disappear if everyone used a computer to keep track of players taken and money remaining. For some reason, many leagues have an unwritten rule forbidding computers in the draft room and some have written rules to that effect. Why? Probably there is that lingering fear of the supernerd, who can leap tall buildings and win any league when he is powered by 2.0 megs of RAM with a souped-up CPU. We say not to worry about it. People are going to use computers extensively, before and after the draft, if that's their inclination. So why slow down the Big Day just because you want to see people doing arithmetic with a pencil and paper. Are real baseball GM's prohibited from using computers? Heck, no!

If you do use a computer program before and during the draft, you want the best, of course. We may be prejudiced, but we honestly believe John's product is far above all the others and many impartial observers are saying the same thing. For information about John Benson's Draft Software, please call 203-834-0812 Monday-Friday.

ROTISSERIE RECOMMENDATION
All questions defining the player pool and position
eligibility should be settled before you begin your
draft or auction.

Under no circumstances should you start playing with the
idea that you can deal with any questions if and when they arise.
Questions most certainly will arise, and if your policy is to be
"democratic" and vote on which players are eligible at which
positions, your league is going to break down into personality
contests and factions before you even get through draft day. This
advice applies to any and all rules interpretations, not just
position eligibility.

You don't have to list every player and every position
(although it wouldn't hurt, if someone is willing to make an
"official" list). You can write clear, general rules such as "must
be on a major league roster or major league disabled list on the
day of the draft to be eligible," and "must have played 20 or
games at the designated position during the previous season." **It
is very important to cite official sources for all rules, especially position eligibility, so that you don't get bogged down
in arguments about whose book is correct.** The Sporting News
Baseball Register, the Sporting News Official Baseball Guide,
and the Baseball America Almanac are some popular authorities
on positions played in the previous year.

If you join the Rotisserie League Baseball Association, one
of the many benefits is a list of eligible players and eligible
positions using RLBA rules. These documents themselves are
worth the price of membership. See chapter 10 for more information on joining.

*If Rotisserie baseball teaches you anything
about life, it gives you an appreciation for having
written rules of conduct.*

4TH INNING

RULES PART III: MANAGING YOUR ROSTER

> *"If you want to get off this team, you have to take a number."*
>
> — *Dave Revering*
> *On the Yankees in 1981*

THE LINEUP

- Should your league allow roster replacements?
- How often should you have free agent drafts during the season?
- What are the advantages of a large reserve list?
- Why is September such a significant time for acquiring minor leaguers?

In the simplest possible fantasy league, your work is done after you have assembled your opening day roster. You can simply check again in October and see which team has the best stats. In real Rotisserie leagues, however, just like real baseball, the season is just beginning in April.

All kinds of problems can (and will) arise after you draft your dream team. In fact, you can be sure that everything conceivable will go wrong. If Rotisserie teaches you anything about life, it is a deep appreciation for Murphy's Law. Your Cy Young pitcher, who was supposed to be the cornerstone of your staff, will blow out his shoulder on a cold April night in Chicago and will be gone for the season. Your superstar outfielder will slip on a bar of soap and break a leg in early May. The rookie who

61

was supposed to be your big sleeper will hit .136 in April, get sent all the way back down to Double-A and will eventually go to Japan. Your one healthy star having a great season will be traded to the other league (e.g. the AL if you're using NL players only) and you will lose him, too. These are the natural events in every unfolding season. Get used to them.

The decision for your league Rules Committee is how forgiving you want to be when everyone's roster starts to come unglued. The most liberal rules allow continuous and unlimited access to the free agent pool. Your player gets hurt? Pick a replacement. Your rookie gets benched? Pick a replacement. You see a new kid getting all the saves in San Diego? Go ahead and claim him anytime, and just throw away your worst pitcher to make room on your roster.

Commercial services that charge transaction fees are likely to favor the "unlimited access" rule when it comes to choosing replacements. Every time you change your mind, for any reason, they get more money. So, why not let you have as much fun as possible, churning your roster all summer? Some of the private leagues also like unlimited access; it's a great way to enlarge the kitty with transaction fees during the summer, if you play for money. Assuming you play in a 12-team league, the limited available talent pool will minimize moves. Sometimes it's just a question of what people think is fun and how much time your league secretary is willing to put into record-keeping.

ROSTER MOVE LIMITS

Most leagues don't allow unlimited roster moves. **There are three principal forms of limitation:**

(1) **Roster moves may be restricted according to the REASON for replacement.** For example, almost all leagues allow replacement picks when a player is formally placed on the Disabled List by his major league team, sent down to the minor leagues, waived, released or traded to a team that makes him ineligible for that particular fantasy league (e.g. the "other

league"). But many leagues draw the line right there: if any player remains "active" on a major league roster, you cannot replace him, even if the player is widely reported to be suffering from blinding headaches and hasn't touched a bat or ball in three weeks.

16. Our league will allow roster moves
☐ when a player is formally placed on the DL by his team
☐ RLBA rules
☐ Other (why) _____

(2) **Roster moves may be restricted according to QUANTITY.** Some leagues allow all the replacements necessary for the reasons stated in (1) above, plus they allow a limited number of "free" discretionary moves. The limited number may be as low as one per year or as high as ten or twenty per year. If you are thinking of a number up around twenty or higher, you may as well allow unlimited moves, and save yourself a great deal of counting. For those leagues that use limits, numbers like three, five and seven are popular.

17. A. We will allow _____
(how many) free roster moves.
B. We will allow _____
(how many) roster moves that cost _____ each.

(3) **Roster moves may be restricted as to TIMING.** In this area, you can become highly creative and league rules can vary widely. Some of the popular variations include:

(a) You may have free agent "re-entry drafts" once or twice per season, or even more frequently. (If you end up having a re-entry draft every week, you really have what amounts to continuous access.) In these drafts, usually going in reverse order of standings, each team drafts a new player and throws away an unwanted one. The drafts may be limited to just one round or they

63

may go endlessly, until every team is satisfied that they have the best possible players, given who is available to choose from. Even if you have a free agent draft as frequently as once a month, there will be plenty of activity, as players come and go from the free agent pool and owners change their minds. Personally,we like re-entry drafts, because they provide a reason for your league to meet as a group, although they can be done by phone.

18. A. Free agent drafts will be held
- ☐ weekly
- ☐ every 2 weeks
- ☐ monthly
- ☐ never
- ☐ other _____

B. The free agent draft will be held
- ☐ at a meeting
- ☐ by phone

(b) You may have a "grace period" lasting a week (or a month) after opening day, when owners are allowed to correct mistakes they made on draft day. For example, let everyone make one or two (or several) changes in their roster, throwing away the veterans who got benched and claiming the youngsters who took their places. After the grace period, you could return to limited moves or restrictions allowing only replacements required by DL status, demotion, etc. as noted in (1) above.

19. Will our league have a "grace period?"
Yes ☐ No ☐ If yes, until what date? _____

(c) You may allow unlimited "free" roster moves up to any specified date, after which changes can only be made when a player is disabled, waived or demoted by his major league team.

The All Star break is a popular cutoff, providing a quiet, three-day period when the numbers stop changing and owners can reflect thoughtfully about their needs.

20. Will we allow unlimited "free" roster moves?
Yes ☐ No ☐ If yes, until what date? _____

(d) You may keep a tight rein on roster moves all year and then declare open season during September. Major league teams are allowed to expand their rosters from 25 to 40 in September every year. Most of the major league rosters add only three or four players (one of numerous reasons for keeping the number low: there simply aren't enough lockers in most clubhouses to accommodate 40 players). The key point is that the best minor leaguers are the ones who get promoted during September. Opening up your league's access to free agents in September will stimulate the interest of teams that have fallen out of your pennant race, especially if you give first access to the teams that are low in the standings. For the contenders, September callups offer the possibility of new blood that can shift a delicate competitive balance in the most fascinating directions.

21. We will allow _____ free
agent acquisitions in September.
The date _____
The cost _____.

By listing all these options and possibilities, we are not trying to confuse you. Indeed, there are many choices to consider and many options not mentioned above. When you start combining one method with another, there are innumerable variations possible. You can make the game as simple as you want, however. For starting a new league, we recommend the following:

Study the official Rotisserie League rules in the Waggoner/ Sklar book. **If your league is following anything close to the** official Rotisserie format in other aspects, use the standard methods for replacements. (Basically, you can reserve and replace players who are disabled, released, traded to the other league, demoted to the minor leagues or otherwise removed from their active major league roster.) First-year leagues may want to try playing without the Free Agent Acquisition Budget (FAAB) and without the September roster expansion as described in the RLBA rules, but after some experience you will see how those rules can add to your enjoyment. Since this volume is aimed primarily at less experienced players, we are not even going to describe those rules here now. The Waggoner/Sklar book explains them beyond our ability to clarify or enhance and we cover them in Volume II anyway.

One note on Disabled Lists and waivers: almost every league allows for replacements in these "necessary" circumstances, and almost every league has problems at some time with a lack of clarity about whether a player is on the DL or isn't. In the world of major league baseball, the problem is real and murky and likely to remain so. Teams often hold informal news briefings in clubhouses or dim corridors after games, making verbal announcements that certain players will be placed on the DL. Is the player then on the DL? Or is the team saying that they INTEND to place the player on the DL the next day or even the day after tomorrow? Only the major league general manager knows for sure. The team is required to notify the league office when they make a move, just like the field manager is required to tell the umpire when he is removing one player and inserting another — but the general manager's communication to the league office is invisible and confidential. The league offices will not disclose what communications they have received, because they deem it a team function to make all public announcements concerning disabilities (and there is a valid reason why: the team usually wants to tell the player himself, before any news of the move reaches the media and the league office can't be expected to know what the teams have told the players or when).

Since there is no official, central clearinghouse for DL information, and since your league secretary cannot reasonably be expected to call every major league team every day to learn who has been placed on the DL (or waived, or whatever), **it is vital that your league adopt a standard definition and an official source.**

Our recommendation is to choose a printed source, such as USA TODAY, so that everyone can look for themselves and see who is disabled and who isn't. USA TODAY prints daily transactions (except Saturday and Sunday) and prints a complete DL for each league every week. If your league wants faster access to information, you can adopt the USA TODAY or STATS, Inc. on-line sports network, or the AP Wire as available on CompuServe. Whatever you choose, however, write into your league rules what the official source shall be, because the media are full of conflicting reports and contradictory "information." Don't let this confusion cause a problem in your league.

If you follow official Rotisserie rules on roster replacements, consider playing without the tight linkage of replacement players to the reserved players whom they replaced. To explain, the RLBA rules (in 1991) provide that a reserved player becomes "married" to his replacement. Suppose you had Kelly Gruber go on the DL, and you managed to grab Dean Palmer as a replacement. When Gruber becomes healthy again, your wish is that you could activate Gruber on your roster, keep the young phenom Palmer, and throw away Randy Velarde who was one of your worst selections on draft day.

In Rotisserie lingo, this example means that you have linked Palmer and Gruber, or you could say you "have Palmer on top of Gruber." You are not allowed to activate Gruber and waive an unproductive player such as Velarde. (If Velarde should become disabled, you could activate Gruber to replace Velarde, but now we're getting into fine points that keep league secretaries awake at night — let them worry about the exceptions to the exceptions.) The basic rule revolves around the fact that you are not allowed to trade Gruber and keep Palmer. You can trade the reserved Gruber and the active Palmer together ("one on top of the other"), and you can trade Palmer for a different replacement, but you cannot use the activation of Gruber to help you get rid of a healthy Velarde.

If all this sounds very complicated, that's because it is very complicated. The whole intent, which has some merit, is that no one should ever benefit from a player getting hurt. If Kelly Gruber is injured, following this line of reasoning, that injury should not create a windfall for Gruber's owner, in the form of an eventual escape from the unhappy circumstance of owning Randy Velarde.

Our preference is to let a re-activated player go into any qualified position and roster spot chosen by his owner, displacing the least-wanted player who can be waived while maintaining a full complement of players at the required positions. In making this reactivation, the owner should be allowed to move players from one position to another, wherever they may be eligible, to maximize the total value remaining on the roster.

Basically, you will find that we like almost any rule that puts more management discretion and more decision-making into the hands of the owner. For example, when an injured player is activated, give the owner a free choice about which player to replace, as long as he sticks to the position requirement. On access to free agents: the more frequently an owner has opportunities to acquire free agents from the pool, the more he can make decisions to shape his roster the way he wants it to be. Shuffling roster spots when someone comes off of the DL can be a fascinating puzzle, remarkably similar to the problem faced by a real major league GM when a disabled player becomes active again. In a Rotisserie format, the choices can be a major source of fun. Do you shift your roster toward power or speed? Do you want to waive the aging veteran who hasn't played in a week, or drop the promising rookie who has tons of potential but is hitting only .180 so far this year?

Allow some limited number of "free" moves. There is

something unnatural and undesirable about an owner who spends the summer wishing that a certain player on his roster should break a leg or get run over by a bus. You can't prevent these thoughts entirely, but you can cut down on their frequency.

Official Rotisserie League rules have a generally punitive treatment of any draft pick or acquisition that turns out to be unwise. The single most frustrating part of roster management in the strict Rotisserie format is the permanence of bad players on your roster, especially when there are good (or not so bad) replacements available in the free agent pool. It is unnatural, but all too common, to see Rotisserie leaguers making trades based on the theme: "If you take this bum off my hands, I will give you a truly valuable player to go along with him; and you give me two mediocre bodies; I just can't stand this guy any more." Such deals shouldn't happen.

The worst aspect of "no mercy" rules concerning replacements, is that owners end up wishing that their weakest players would get injured or demoted to the minors, so the owner has a legal reason to choose a replacement. Another unnatural result is that the almost-mediocre players usually cause more suffering than do the players who are really very bad.

Consider the case of two owners, each drafting a rookie. One of the youngsters hits .190 in April and obviously can't handle major league pitching; he gets sent back to the minors, and his owner gets to choose a replacement. The other rookie hits .220 all year, with 0 HR and 9 RBI, just good enough to stay in the major leagues, but bad enough to kill his owner's team batting average while offering nothing of value in the other categories.

So it can happen that the owner who makes a truly rotten pick gets a reprieve, in the form of a second chance, while the owner who picks a mediocre rookie, good enough to stick in the major leagues all year, ends up suffering more — and he never has the option of choosing a replacement. Whenever you take away management discretion, or create situations where worse decisions lead to better results, you create more possibilities for underserved outcomes.

You don't want a league where most of the owners end up hating their players. The more owners feel that they have control over their rosters, the more they will enjoy the game, and the more skill will enter into the determination of a winner. I am not suggesting a totally forgiving attitude toward bad picks. We have already discussed methods to limit and restrict owners' powers to undo their worst selections.

You can pick and choose a suitable combination of limits concerning when replacements can be chosen, and how many "free" moves may be granted. You can also charge an outrageous price for these discretionary moves, and make people enrich the kitty (if you play for money) when they want to undo a bad decision. Our advice, nonetheless, is that you should provide SOME outlet for owners to rid themselves of their worst player or players. It is a real good feeling to imagine calling the player into your office and saying, "Things just haven't worked out; you're gone!" and crossing his name off your list.

To summarize our recommendations on player replacements:

(1) **Generally follow the RLBA methods** unless you have a good reason to do something different. It is always helpful to have an official source giving you definitions and examples.

(2) **Add a little flexibility to the rules for players being reactivated from the DL.** The RLBA rules tying DL players and replacements together, are complex, confining, and (in the end) beatable through clever loopholes anyway.

(3) **Provide some kind of option to get rid of players who are performing poorly,** even if the option is to allow just one move per year and that move costs a fortune.

(4) As a general theme, if you are in doubt about any specific rule concerning replacements, **opt for the choice that gives each owner more power and control of his roster.**

REPLACEMENTS AND RESERVE LISTS

All of the above discussion is based on a simple roster, with all players active and counting toward their Rotisserie team's stats. In the above rules provisions, there is no reserve list or farm system except for the small number of disabled or demoted players who have been retained by their owners, while temporary replacement picks are accumulating numbers on the active rosters.

Numerous problems concerning replacements, disabilities, waivers, and corrections of bad picks can be prevented or fixed by the creation of a fairly large reserve list or farm system for each team in your league. For example, in the highest and most complex form of official Rotisserie rules, called "Rotisserie Ultra," every team owns 40 players throughout the season, and owners make weekly decisions about which players shall be active and which shall be held on the Reserve Roster. The Ultra format (discussed in Volume II) provides for 23 players to be active, at the usual required positions, and 17 players (any position) be held on reserve. The stats of the active players count toward team totals each week, while the stats of the reserve players don't figure into the standings in any way.

You don't have to be an "advanced" or Ultra league to get the benefits of a large reserve list. We have already mentioned some of the benefits of any league having a reserve list list or farm system, for example, a 23-man active roster and a 17-man reserve list for each team. **To recap and elaborate the reasons in favor of a large reserve list:**

1. In a league with a small number of teams or a league that uses both AL and NL players, **the reserve list helps to remove talent from the available pool.** You don't want your league's available pool to be too large or too rich with talent, because that would discourage trading (whatever kind of player you need would always be available among the free agents). An excess of available talent often makes owners wish for injuries or demotions, so they can get access to the available pool.

71

2. The reserve list allows a wider range of skills and effort among the owners, without destroying the competitive balance. Owners who don't have too much time, or don't want to get too deeply involved, can assemble credible active rosters using major league regulars and names that everyone recognizes. The more competitive owners can then dig deep into their research and scouting reports, and come up with obscure players that wouldn't come up during a normal draft or auction, but might end up on their reserve list. In the long run, the more serious competitors gain an advantange (it's called "bench strength") — but with good luck, a less serious owner can assemble a good active roster, and if his players stay healthy all year, he can win a league (or at least finish near the top) without a reserve list that reaches deep into the minor leagues.

3. Reserve lists encourage trading. We already stated the fact that reserve lists make for smaller free agent pools, and tiny free agent pools send owners looking for trades when they have a particular need. But there is another reason why reserve lists facilitate trading; the more players you have, the easier it is to "make change." If I have a player worth $25, and you have a player worth $30, and we both want to trade, we may have trouble finding a way for me to compensate you for the difference in value. Normally, in such a trade situation, we would try to find two other players to put into the package (say, I give you the $25 player plus another worth $10, and you give me the $30 player and another worth $5) and we're both happy. Finding "balancing" factors for trades, both in terms of player value and in terms of position eligibility, is much easier when you have 80 players to consider, not just 46.

4. Reserve lists provide a frontier of knowledge and opportunity. Most people are reluctant to perform radical experiments with their active roster, such as putting extreme emphasis on one stat category or one type of player. Rarely does anyone assemble a roster made up entirely of young speedsters or old power hitters, or loaded with strong pitching at the expense of hitting. But with a long reserve list, people can try esoteric

72

strategies like cornering the market on catchers, drafting every possible setup reliever, taking a dozen players all age 24, etc. The reserve list is a great window of opportunity to see the answers to numerous "what if..." questions. It's fun, and it's educational.

5. Finally (the point that got us started on this subject a couple hundred words ago), **reserve lists enhance each owner's real and perceived control of his roster,** especially when it comes to making replacements. Your catcher got hurt? Bring up someone from your reserve list. You have plenty of wins but not enough saves? Put a couple of your starters on reserve, and activate some bullpen types. The most benefit from a reserve list comes when you allow unlimited "shuttle" moves (say, at weekly intervals), let owners de-activate players whenever they see fit and bring up replacements of their own choosing.

ROTISSERIE RECOMMENDATION
Don't let replacements cancel past performance.

Before we leave the subject of replacements, let's go back and consider the most basic contest to see who can pick the best players in April: you just check in again in October and see who has the best statistics. Along this line of thinking, you may be tempted to consider the simplest possible rule for replacements: you might want to let your owners change their rosters during the summer, but still determine the winner based solely on the stats of the players who are left on the active roster when the season ends. The implication of such a rule is that you would "throw away" the stats of any players who are removed during the season, and you would pick up (retroactively) the year-to-date stats of players who are acquired during the summer.

The "simplest possible" method for handling replacements is to pretend that all players on the roster at the end of the year were on the roster as of Opening Day, when you started your contest. You simply look in the newspaper after the season ends, and take the final, full-year stats for every player on every roster. **If you like simplicity, here is some simple advice: don't do it!**

The impact of just one replacement, when you have "all or nothing" accounting for each player's annual performance, can be wild swings in the standings, especially when replacement picks are made in July or August or (shudder) September. If you have a tight pennant race, it will be ruined; no one will know where any team stands until the final rosters are settled. The standings you are following through May, June and July will be silly, meaningless pro-forma forecasts based on the assumption that rosters will never change: "If the rosters stay the same as they are today, then the standings as of today would be . . ." And then when you allow replacements, that premise becomes completely invalid, and the standings you have been studying will become meaningless or even damaging.

Many of the most casual leagues still employ this simplistic approach to roster changes. We have played in such a league and hated it, even when we finished first. Throwing away just one bad pitcher in August, and seeing all those earned runs, hits and walks being erased from history like an episode in a George Orwell novel will make your head spin. When several replacements occur, the result is to create a whole new league. Leading teams can drop all the way to the bottom, while low-standing teams can soar to the top, all in one evening.

With retroactive credit for free agents acquired in mid season and complete forgiveness of bad numbers attached to players who are thrown away, the ethical perversion is this: the teams that made the worst selections and have the worst players on their rosters have the most to gain when they are allowed access to the free agent pool. Combine that fact with the common practice of giving low-standing teams first access to the free agent pool when it's time to choose replacements, and you can see why some competitors in the "full year stat" leagues will deliberately put bad players on their rosters in April and May, ensuring priority access to free agents during the season, then throw away their bums at the last possible moment and see the

74

bums' bad numbers go away with them. And when you consider the cataclysmic impact of multi-player trades in such an environment, well, it makes you want to call the Rotisserie Police!

We understand the arguments in favor of "full year" stat-keeping. Your league secretary doesn't have time to keep adding and subtracting stats from players who come and go from various rosters during the summer. Maybe you don't even want to buy a paper every week to keep the necessary information on file. And you don't want to spend money on a professional stat service. So it is elegantly simple just to say, "We will look in the paper after the season ends, and see who picked the best team." If you want simplicity, there are better alternatives, preserving some semblance of a meaningful contest.

Consider the following possibilities:

(1) **Simply don't allow any changes, replacements, or trades during the season.** Doesn't sound like much fun? OK, how about . . .

(2) **Make all changes (trades, replacements, etc.) take effect as of the All Star break.** You can certainly afford to buy one newspaper during the summer, and your secretary should have enough time to separate the stats of a few players into "first half" and "second half," and see that the right numbers go the right teams.

(3) **Use a stat service, so you can allow as many changes as your league prefers** without driving your secretary crazy.

There is nothing more satisfying than making a trade that brings a championship to your team. There is also nothing that makes you feel worse than a trade that proves to be disastrous.

5TH INNING

RULES PART IV:
TRADES AND RETENTIONS

> *"If I knew then what I know now, I wouldn't have made the trade. But if I knew what I know now, I wouldn't have voted for Richard Nixon."* — *Hank Peters*
>
> *As the Orioles general manager who traded for Reggie Jackson, only to see him become a free agent and leave the club*

THE LINEUP

- How much trading should our league allow?
- How can lopsides trades undermine the balance of the league and cause majro problems?
- How many players should we be allowed to retain each year?
- Should we have long-term contracts?

TRADE REGULATIONS

Trading raises Rotisserie ownership to its highest level. Within the game of roster management, piecing together the architecture of a multi-player deal is infinitely more complex than simply making a draft pick. Both sides must assess the multiple variables and ranges of probabilities, and conclude that the change in personnel will improve the total value of the franchise — not an easy conclusion to reach.

Within the "fantasy" aspect, there is a definite feeling of power when you remove one multi-million-dollar athlete from your stable and replace him with another. Personally, we get a bigger charge out of the outright release with its punitive undertones, but trading is a close second. Without trading, the game wouldn't be nearly as much fun.

Trading is a complex subject that could fill numerous volumes. Indeed, when we get into the strategy and tactics section of this book, you will find that we have plenty to say about player swapping and the related world of negotiation and deal-making. For the time being, our recommendations will focus on rules to provide a framework for your league's wheeling and dealing.

Rules about trading? "Why have rules about trading?" you may ask. Superficially, it may seem that "anything goes" should be the motto of every Rotisserie league. Indeed, many leagues start with this premise. **Veteran players can tell you, however, that trading is unquestionably the source of the most contentious disagreements in every league and is the single greatest cause of league disintegration due to hard feelings.** You may decide, after careful consideration, to take a hands-off attitude toward trades in your league, but you had better think about the question before reaching this conclusion.

ROTISSERIE RECOMMENDATION

Give very careful consideration to your trade policies to avoid arguments and hard feelings among the owners. This cannot be stressed too much.

HOW MUCH LATITUDE?

The central problem is that trading raises the possibility that one team can help another team. Imagine a foot race where the slowest runner, halfway around the track, can find a way to take away 30 yards from his own position and present this distance as a gift to one of the frontrunners. How would you feel if you were a contender huffing and puffing toward the finish line when suddenly your closest rival shoots 90 feet forward and ends the race instantly?! Such is the stuff of Rotisserie trade controversies. It is no consolation to know that the gift-giver dropped farther back after helping his friend win the race.

Your league's trade rules will have to fit the style and disposition of your individual league owners. Using the "regular poker group" analogy, some leagues will choose to be close-to-the-vest and formal, while others tend to be permissive and even raucous in their attitudes toward decorum and the rights of the individual.

If your league was founded as a break-away group that left another league because they found trade restrictions (or complaints) spoiled their fun, you may write league rules stating explicitly: "anything goes," and spend the whole summer seeing who can engineer the most collusive trade with the biggest impact. (We don't recommend that, but we know some people who think along those lines.) At the other end of the spectrum, if you want the tightest possible methods to maintain the balance of power that existed at the end of your of your draft or auction, you might want to rule out trading completely. (We don't recommend that, either, but again, we know some people who think that way, also.)

BASIC TRADING GUIDELINES

Our advice is that every league should have a serious discussion about what you want to tolerate in terms of free trade (there is no substitute for communication) before writing any rules about trades. Then and follow these basic guidelines when you formulate your rules:

(1) State your league philosophy, in brief and general terms, in writing. Be explicit. For example: "The league recognizes that trading creates an opportunity for one team to help another, make two weak rosters into one strong team, etc. Lopsided trades that help one team at the expense of another are not in the best interest of enjoyable fair play and will not be tolerated."

79

(2) When writing a general rule to prohibit lopsided trades, **don't waste your time trying to come up with a definition of "lopsided."** Being explicit doesn't mean you have to be detailed or legalistic. The more details you put into a definition or prohibition, the more loopholes and arguments you will create. Having said simply, "lopsided trades will not be tolerated," you don't want to spend the rest of your summer arguing about what lopsided means. It doesn't take a genius to recognize a lopsided trade for what it is. Some simple methods of detection and enforcement are discussed below.

(3) Have a trading deadline. The worst trades occur after one of the two parties has given up the race or, even worse, lost interest in the league completely. In April and May, almost everyone is optimistic. In June, a few people begin to have doubts, but not until July or August does any real despair set in. The official Rotisserie League trade deadline is July 31. You might want to move that forward (say, to the All Star break) but you don't want to move it back. Most of the trades that have led to bloodshed have been conceived and executed during mid-August. Don't take chances.

(4) Require that trades leave every roster whole and legal. Specifically, prohibit trades that leave any roster spot open at any required position, even if the vacant slot is intended to be filled within the next few minutes. The owner with the incomplete roster may swear on his children's souls that he has another trade on the verge of completion and that he will surely restore his roster before the beginning of the next stat-keeping period. Don't believe him. If there is a three-way deal in the works, force the three teams to consummate a complete deal that leaves every team with a whole and legal roster and present the deal in its entirety.

(5) Require that all trades involve only players for players. Specifically, prohibit deals involving future draft picks, money (either real cash or imaginary "auction" money) or any future promises. Complicated deals, even if they are clearly defined and presented in writing to the league secretary, place an unfair burden on the league to administer. Your league secretary can be expected to keep records showing which players belong to which teams, but he cannot be expected to function as a collection agency or arbiter.

Imagine the chaos that will result when someone calls the league secretary in September and says, "That bastard never paid me the $10 he promised, so the deal we made back in June is hereby canceled!" Another illustration (we actually saw this happen): someone jumps up in the middle of an auction, yelling, "He promised not to bid over $22 for Roberto Kelly if I traded him Rickey Henderson for Ruben Sierra last winter. He promised! It was part of the deal; that bid is illegal!" Do everyone a favor and make it clear that your league does not record any trades except, simply, Player A and Player B for Player C and D.

WHEN CHARLIE FINLEY MEETS
GEORGE STEINBRENNER

> *"You always dream of trading for the perfect player.*
> *But you can't, because if an excellent player*
> *isn't scarred in some way, you don't*
> *get a chance to trade for them."*
> — *Frank Cashen, Met General Manager*

Concerning enforcement of the "no lopsided trades" rule, we can recommend two simple methods:

(1) You might select an outside independent authority to act as arbiter. It is perfectly OK to have a "commissioner" as long as that person has no interest in your league or its participants. A veteran owner from another league, someone who can be nominated and approved before the season starts (and written into the rules!) will usually meet your needs. You can always call John on his 900 number. He will be glad to listen to any question and express his opinion. He has probably saved a couple of leagues from disintegrating into fistfights.

(2) Keeping everything within your league family, you could adopt what we call the "three-owner doomsday veto"

rule. Stated briefly, this rule provides that if any three owners believe that a trade is too lopsided to be a credible, good-faith bargain, they may jointly veto the trade AFTER listening to the explanations and reasoning of the trading parties. we call this a "doomsday" rule because it goes on to require that the three owners put their veto into the form of a letter concluding: "We find you guilty of bad sportsmanship." Obviously, the league might experience some signs of a schism after that letter gets mailed.

The nice thing about this rule is that it tends to be self-policing. When you write it into the rules, everyone understands and agrees that lopsided deals will not be tolerated. we have played in a couple of leagues that use such a rule and we believe that whenever trade negotiations take a lopsided turn, one party or the other will get that "uh oh" feeling that the trade is too unbalanced. In my experience, the rule has never had to be invoked.

(3) Finally, one method you don't want to use: don't ask the league to vote on any question like whether a trade is lopsided. If three people smell a rat, that's enough to confirm the presence of a large rodent. One person might have a paranoid imagination; he might even find a friend to agree with him. It is highly unlikely that three people will all hallucinate simultaneously. (If your league does have three crazy people, you are going to have a problem eventually anyway, so you might as well bring it to the surface with the simple undoing of a trade.) If you start politicking and voting on these things, your "fairness" rule is going to break down into a popularity contest. You will end up with two leagues eventually, so you might as well start out that way.

PLAYER DUMPING

Dumping is a special case of a lopsided trade, where both parties are working from selfish, competitive motives. This special situation doesn't exactly fit the model of one team trying to help another. It's more like, "You help my team this year and I'll help your team next year." The reasons and motivations for player-dumping are connected to the rules concerning player retentions, so you might want to look at the section on Retentions, if you find that anything in the following discussion makes you ask yourself questions like, "Why would anyone do such a thing?"

Very often, a team which is clearly out of contention when the trading deadline nears will give up on the current season and start building for the future. The non-contending team suddenly becomes willing to let go of valuable players that don't fit into their future plans. For example, any players who cannot legally be retained at the end of the season have no value to a team focused solely on "next year." Other players may be unattractive to the non-contenders because they have high salaries, because they are aging veterans in danger of losing playing time within a year or two or because they are rumored to be going to the "other league" via trade or free agency during the coming winter.

The natural self-interest of the non-contending team is to get something of value for the players who don't figure into their future plans. What do the non-contenders want in return? Any developing youngster with a likelihood of improved performance in the coming season would be good trade bait. Any player with a low salary would be attractive to the owner focused on next year. If the league allows trading of minor league players, draft picks, etc., all of these little assets, which wouldn't likely help a contender during the pennant stretch, could be of great interest to a team that has fallen by the wayside.

Now look at this question from the point of view of a contender. One star player might be enough to put you over the top. Two star players could put the championship on ice. In the heat of a pennant race, you just want pure talent and on-field performance now, without reference to salary level, contract status or any other factor affecting "next year." And a team fighting for a place at the top of the standings usually isn't going to be too concerned about building for next year. Younger developing talents, players with low salaries and other future considerations are going to get minimal attention.

Thus we get the perfect circumstances for a trade that helps both teams: the low-standing owner trades away his two highest-paid, superstar players [their salaries being so high that no one would consider keeping them at such prices — that's one reason why the team is near the bottom of the league] and in return he gets two low-salaried, highly-touted youngsters who aren't doing much this year, but are likely to blossom into stars during spring training next year. The non-contender may drop from seventh to tenth place by making this trade, but what does he care? The excitement is at the other end of the standings where the third place team (for example) gets the two superstars and rises to first place. How would you feel if you were one of the two teams that got passed during this process? We can tell exactly how you would feel: angry.

In these late-season cases of player dumping, trades can be so momentous that they undo the original intent of the contest: To see who can pick the best players in a draft or auction. Any veteran Rotisserian will tell you that first place often goes to the owner who can best sweet talk the low-standing teams into giving up the fight and dumping their star players into the hands of a sympathetic bystander. Trading has its place in the process of roster management, but most leagues don't want to turn the whole contest into a game of "let's make a deal."

Thus we get to the anti-dumping rules. The original Rotisserie League, as usual, sets the standard for the most elegantly complex treatment of every conceivable situation. The RLBA rule creates a class of "asterisk players," defined as those who have salaries over $25 or those who will become free agents at the end of the current season (by finishing a long term contract or by playing out their option year). This group naturally includes most of the players who would be shipped to contending teams in deals that could be characterized as player-dumping.

Having defined the category of players that shouldn't be dumped, the official rules then include the requirements for treating those players, to prevent dumping. Specifically: **For each asterisk player traded during the season, an asterisk player must be received in return, except that once during each season one asterisk player may be traded without receiving an asterisk player in return.**

This anti-dumping rule is a step in the right direction, but it moves along the edge of a precipice. The problem is this: when you explain in detail exactly what is NOT permitted, you implicitly define exactly what IS permitted. If you push your imagination just a little, you can easily conjure up a scenario of extreme player-dumping that falls outside the intent of anti-dumping rules (for example, injured asterisk players could be included in a trade). The unpleasant result is that you still have player-dumping and the perpetrators can now point to the rules and say, "What we are doing is perfectly legal; it says so in the rules!"

John B: In all areas of rule-making, I recommend simplicity and in those areas of conduct that are most likely to result in hard feelings and accusations of bad sportsmanship, my recommendation is to make your rules as general as possible. State the spirit of the law clearly and you are less likely to see that spirit violated.

CompuServe Sports Forum has produced some of the best language that I have ever seen for dealing with the problem of player-dumping (and lopsided trades in general). Consider the following provisions:

A trade which has a "substantial inequity in the exchange of talent or is otherwise substantially detrimental to the league" is not permitted, "regardless of the value of the trade to the trading parties."

The current season is the principle concern, regardless of the date and nature of a trade.

The overriding question is not whether a trade is fair to the parties involved, but whether it is fair to the remaining members of the league.

Randy B: Player dumping is certainly an area that each league needs to discuss in detail. Many leagues feel that dumping is perfectly legitimate, as long as anti-dumping rules (such as the asterisk rule) are followed. Other leagues feel that each owner has an obligation not to dump his players, not to receive dumped players in return, and to avoid lopsided trades to build for the future. The important thing is to decide what is preferred by the owners in each league to avoid problems.

John B: If you allow this type of trading (dumping), be aware that some people perceive it as collusion even if the two people did not get together to make a plot, "I am going to help you this year — you help me next year." Some owners will be angry if someone trades stars and gets back one dollar players.

Randy B: However, if the league feels such trades are acceptable, then playing for next year is fine.

John B: This is the number one area where there are arguments in leagues. Even when people do not intend to be colluding, it might look like that after the trade is done. Take this into consideration when you design your rules. You should realize that even if everyone behaves appropriately, the rules may creat a situation where people end up unhappy.

I think you have a moral obligation to the league not to make lopsided trades, even if it is within the rules.

Randy B: The real problem occurs because owners have different purposes — the game lasts for one year and in theory, you are trying to win this year. People trying to win now will have their outcome affected by owners who are not playing that game, but who are trying to build for the future. They are not playing "pick the best team this year"; they are playing "pick the best team for next year or the year after next."

So if you design rules to make it very hard to play for the future, then I think it is all right to play for next year.

John B: I would steer the rules toward winning this year; many leagues write into their constitution that the evaluation of whether a trade is fair is based on this year's impact on the league.

Randy B: That's a good idea. Make sure that everyone understands all of the rules so you do not have a trade on July 31 that has everyone complaining. The owners should realize that you either have:
1. No dumping
2. A little dumping
3. A free-for-all

John B: Here's another thought . . . You cannot make a rule against stupidity. You can appeal to the conscience of owners not to take advantage of other owners who are not so skillful, but you cannot put in a rule that someone is not allowed to make a stupid trade.

Randy B: In one of my leagues, the only trades allowed after the all star break are between teams next to each other in the standings. This eliminates the problem when a first division team trades for this year and a second division team is looking toward the future.

We also have a rule that any players traded during the season have their salary increase to a minimum of $10 automatically.

John B: I think those are excellent rules. I also love in season salary caps. For example, in a $260 league, a maximum of $360 per team works well. If you have such a rule, it means that the total salary of all of your players cannot add up to more than $360. If you have a lot of $10 pickups during the summer, you can get up to $360 pretty easily.

Randy B: Any rule that raises salaries after a trade is good, because it prevents the inexpensive players that become the bait for dumping.

John B: I like having a trade deadline of September 1, so during the stretch drive the winner is decided by the current rosters (plus any free agent or minor league acquisitions).

22. Trading Policy:

Yes ☐ No* ☐ A: Teams are allowed to make trades of any kind throughout the year.

B: Teams are allowed to make trades with the following restrictions:

Yes* ☐ No ☐ From July 31 — August 31, trades may take place only between teams next to each other in the preceding week's standings.

Yes* ☐ No ☐ From September 1 — end of the season, no trades are allowed.

Yes* ☐ No ☐ Trades must be made position for position (P + OF for P + OF) during the season.

Trades made in the off season are ☐ bound ☐ not bound* by the position requirements.

Trades ☐ change ☐ do not change salaries of players. Explain any changes. _____

_____

Trades ☐ do ☐ do not affect the contract status of players.

Yes* ☐ No ☐ Trades prohibit "players to be named later" and "future considerations."

Yes* ☐ No ☐ Trades are subject to the anti-dumping rules in
the official Rotisserie rules. See the book.

Yes* ☐ No ☐ Trades must be for the same number of players
(1 for 1, 2 for 2, etc.)

23. Trades are subject to a fee of _____.

RETENTIONS

In the simplest possible contest to pick players, the game
ends when the season ends. Many leagues with elaborate rules in
other areas stick to this simple idea and turn all players loose at
the end of each season. **Most leagues, however, allow their
owners to keep some number of players from year to year,
better fulfilling the definition of ownership.**

**There is good reason to provide for continuity in your
league's rosters from year to year.** After rooting for your
players through a whole season, you get used to them. You know
which box scores are most worthy of examination every morning; you even know where in the lineup your players are likely
to appear. After 162 games, your eyes are trained to elicit the
necessary information speedily. Indeed, any experienced player
will tell you that one of the difficult aspects of beginning any new
season is the strangeness of new names in new locations in the
daily box scores.

Some critics of Rotisserie leagues complain that the game
undermines "fan loyalty." There is some truth in this statement,
but it would be far more accurate to say that fan loyalty shifts
away from team loyalty and toward player loyalty. Rotisserie
enthusiasts get more excited about their players than anyone,
except possibly youngsters who make players into personal
idols.

And we could make a strong case that Rotisserians are right
up there with the kids when it comes to loving one player or
hating another. We remember one owner who had Mark McGwire

(the 49 homer rookie) in 1987 and this fellow would greet me every morning (it seemed like every morning) by coming into my office, swinging an imaginary bat, pointing to an imaginary outfield fence, and exclaiming, "Mark McGwire! Mark McGwire!"

Rotisserians have their favorite players and it enhances their enjoyment to start each year with a core of returning veterans. After a year of rooting passionately for a player to do well, it can be painful to see him on someone else's roster. So you might wonder: why not just let every owner keep every player from year to year and cut them loose only when they feel like it?

The obvious problem with permanent retentions is the dynasty syndrome. A league ceases to be fun after two or three years when the same team wins every year and you know who is going to win before the season even begins. Many leagues get started with one or two knowledgeable players pulling in eight or ten suckers and the two experienced guys take all the best players. You need some method to ensure that top players get recycled from time to time and you have to offer hope that any team can win in any year. If your league doesn't yet address the issue of keeping players "forever," start working on it now.

There are two methods to prevent the emergence of boring dynasties: (1) You can limit the number of players who can be kept each year and (2) you can attach escalating salaries to all players, if you draft your players using an auction format.

Both the fixed salary budget and the fixed number of allowed retentions will help bring talent back into the available pool year after year. The standard Rotisserie retention limit is 15 players, although many leagues establish their own limits such as 10, 12 or 16. Obviously, the smaller the number of retentions allowed, the more players will be coming back into the pool each year. Also note that most leagues have a minimum number of retentions; the standard is seven who must be retained by every team each year.

The standard Rotisserie rules (seven players minimum, fifteen players maximum) are the most popular method for handling retentions. The salary treatment is a little complicated, especially when compared to the popular alternatives, but the people who invented the game have a great deal of insight into what is enjoyable (and a great deal of knowledge about what works), so their method is worth a little study before you decide what your league should do.

Every player starts with an acquisition salary, usually the price paid in auction. (Other sources of starting salaries are assigned salaries for midseason callups — usually $10 — and "sealed bid" salaries from free agent acquisitions.) Take a simple case and assume you buy a player at auction for $9. **Your retention rights are as follows:**

(1) You may keep the player for another year at the same salary, $9. You may, of course, release the player and then have the option of bidding on him in the next year's auction, just like all the other owners may bid on him.

(2) After two years at the same (original) salary, you have three choices about what to do with player in the third year:

(a) You can release him as noted in (1) above, or

(b) You can sign him for one more year (but only one more year) at the same salary of $9, but then he must be released at the end of the year (the third year is called the "option year") or

(c) You may give the player a raise and sign him to a long term contract. The long term contract price is equal to the original salary plus $5 for each year of the contract. For example, if you have a $9 player and want to keep him for three more years, his salary is $24 per year ($9 plus 3 X $5).

If the official method sounds a little complicated, there is a silver lining: as a new league, you will have over two years to get used to it, before the long term contract provisions

become a factor.

The first year you just have an auction. In the second year, you keep the players you want at their old salaries and throw away the ones who look too expensive. By the time you get to spring training of the third year, you will have had plenty of time to figure out how the long-term contract provisions are going to work. So don't reject this method just because you fear having to study labor law in night school before you can play. Like many things in life, it takes the rules awhile to mature to the point of complexity.

One minor drawback of the standard Rotisserie method, compared to some of the simpler alternatives, is that it keeps your league secretary rather busy. Someone has got to keep track of the status of every player: how he was acquired, how long he has been owned and his status for the coming year. You don't want Cecil Fielder's option year to come and go, with no one remembering that he has to get a long term contract or be released. The record-keeping is genuinely onerous, although league secretaries do have a slight tendency to exaggerate when you ask them about it.

Finally, note that in the Rotisserie salary/contract format, a player's status doesn't change in most leagues when the player is traded from one Rotisserie roster to another. You can't buy Cecil Fielder for $9 in April 1990, hold him for two years plus an option year at $9 and then trade him in the middle of the third year to a new owner who gets to start the clock over again. Option years and contract expiration depend on the calendar, regardless of changes in ownership.

If you want to try a simpler variation of the $260 auction with player salaries escalating gradually and periodically after you acquire them, there are some easy alternatives. The simplest is the once-a-year fixed raise method: you add $4 (or $5) to each player's salary each year and keep going until you reach a year when the player isn't worth keeping. So if you hit the jackpot by acquiring Cecil Fielder for $9 in 1990, you could have retained him for $13 in 1991, $17 in 1992, $21 in 1993, etc.

Cecil Fielder is an extreme case. Very few players are worth $30 to $40 and only very rarely does one of them slip through an auction at a fraction of his value. The $4 per year increase will normally push any player back into the free agent pool within one or two years after he is acquired at a favorable price; if you get a player worth keeping for more than a couple of years, you have an anomaly. In fact, adding $4 to every player's salary every year will make it difficult for many teams to find seven players worth keeping in some years. The players who get squeezed back into the auction year after year are usually those who got purchased for $1 or $2.

The whole issue of retentions and dynasty-busting is one of the major reasons why people choose the auction method rather than a simple draft. The retentions actually start the auction cycle over again, as each team uses part of its $260 budget to retain players from the previous season. If you keep ten players at salaries totaling $130, that means you have spent half your money before the auction even starts.

If you don't use the auction method, you need some other way to get talented players coming back into the pool every year. The maximum retention number helps and if you use the draft method rather than the auction method, you probably want a maximum around 11 or 12, rather than 15. Also, you need some other device, because with ten teams keeping ten players each, there aren't going to be too many superstars among the players cut loose at the end of each season.

If you follow the draft format, one simple idea is to put a time limit on the retention period (three years, for example). The person who drafted Cecil Fielder in the fifteenth round in 1990 thus gets to enjoy Cecil through 1992, but then has to throw him back.

The length-of-service limit can be elaborate, too. Instead of putting a three year limit on every player, you could say (for example) that first round picks may be kept for five years; second, third and fourth round picks can be retained for four years; and fifth through tenth round picks could be retainable for three years, with all other players getting one-year contracts plus an option for one year.

You can put another wrinkle into the contract period by making the long-term players "unwaivable" during the terms of their contracts. If you have to keep a player for five years, you need a pretty good crystal ball to know who is going to keep performing at a high level for a long time.

Randy B: In my favorite league, we have a very simple but fair method of retentions. A player may be retained only for two years (the second year is at a 10% increase in salary from the first year).

The third year the player must be thrown back into the pool unless you keep TOPPERS' RIGHTS on the player. This Topper right in the auction allows you to not bid on the player. When the bidding is completed you may top the last bid by $1 if you wish to keep that player for one more year.

Limiting ownership to two years plus one Toppers' year makes it difficult for a team to build a dynasty, but you can retain a player for the third year if you want him badly. Toppers' rights also add a fascinating new dimension to the auction.

Toppers' rights have value and can be traded during the season or off season. (For a full explanation of Toppers' rights Peter Golenbock's "How to Win at Rotisserie Baseball" is the best source.)

RETENTIONS WITH NO SALARIES AND NO AUCTIONS

If you follow the basic Rotisserie auction, you can always turn to the official rulebook for ideas and models for dealing with every issue. If you don't have an auction or salaries, however, you will need to reinvent the wheel when it comes to dealing with player retentions. The RLBA rules handle the dynasty question with the combination of escalating salaries and the auction format for drafting players each year.

Without salaries, you need another way to deal with the

problems that occur when dominant teams are allowed to keep their best players forever. The following is one attempt at a comprehensive set of rules to address this situation. Using these methods for contract terms in a simple draft format, every player will come back into the free agent pool once every five years and all but a few players will become free agents every couple of years.

1. After the league's first year (or at the end of the first year after this rule is adopted) each team shall be allowed to assign long-term contracts as follows: one player may be signed for five years (not including the year just completed); two players for four years; three players for three years; and four players for two years. Five additional players may be kept for one more "option" year. All of these retentions and contracts are at the discretion of the owner, except that a minimum of five players must be retained every year. The contracts shall be announced when retentions are announced and become irrevocable at that point.

2. Players must be retained every year during their contract terms. Every player's contract is classified according to his year of free agency. For example, if you sign Barry Bonds to a five-year contract at the end of 1992, he must be retained for the five years 1993-1997. Trading a player does not change his contract period, so Bonds becomes a free agent after the 1997 season, regardless who owns him. On league rosters and reports, he would be listed as "Barry Bonds - 97." An option year player would be described as "John Bimbleman - O" for example. Option year players should be separated from midseason pick-ups, because . . .

3. At the end of his option year, a player gets one of three dispositions:

(a) He may be signed to a long-term contract, taking the place of a player whose long-term contract has just expired, for the same term as the expired contract. For example, when Bonds' contract expires after the 1997 season in the above example, another player may be awarded a contract for 1998-2002. When a two-year player contract expires, another player not already having a long-term contract (an option year player or a current year pickup) may be awarded a two-year contract. Or:

(b) The option year a player may be retained for one (and only one) additional year by his current owner. If an option year player is thus retained at the end of the 1992 season, he becomes (for example) "John Bimbleman - 93" and then has a one-year contract. He must be released at the end of his contract period, the same as any long-term player whose contract has expired. Or:

(c) An option year player may be released at the end of his option year.

Note: at the end of a league's first year under these rules, there will be no expiring long-term contracts, and thus no long-term opportunities to sign option year players and midseason pickups to long term contracts. At the end of a league's second year under these rules, the two-year contracts will all expire and two-year contracts may then be assigned to new players to replace them. In future years, all long-term contracts will be expiring, in phases which may overlap. After the fourth year, for example, the four-year players become free agents along with the two-year players who replaced the original two-year players. The point is, it pays to think ahead more than one year when deciding contract status.

4. Injured and retired players and those traded to the Other League may be placed on reserve, but may not be released until their contracts expire, except that any player may be released from a long-term contract upon payment of $100 to the league treasury. When a long-term contract is thus terminated, a new player not already on a long-term contract must be assigned the remainder of the released player's contract.

Note: the $100 fee is intended to be a punitive amount. The $100 represents about 40% of an annual auction budget of a "standard" league, if the league used the auction method. If your league is intended to be about average on the spending scale (roughly equivalent to the $260 auction budget), then $100 should be about right for punitive measures of this type. If your league plays for different prices, then you could adjust the $100 fee accordingly. If you play for fun only, you can use a punitive measure such as removing a team's first three picks in the next draft and replacing them with three picks to be made after all other teams have made all their picks.

5. Contract status does not change at any time except when teams announce their annual retentions (the "Freeze Day") which would normally be about one week before draft day, but could be any time before the season starts. The only changes that could be made at this time would be:

• giving long-term contracts to new players to replace the long-term contracts that have expired,

• awarding one-year contracts to players whose option year has expired,

• selecting new players to be designated as option year players, or

• buying out unexpired long-term contracts and designating replacements to complete the contract periods.

During winter trading and right up until freeze day, all contracts remain unchanged. Players whose long-term contracts have expired are free agents and may not be traded. (This point may seem trivial, but the value of having an expired contract is that it empowers the holder of that contract to award a new long-term contract to another player on Freeze Day.)

6. All players retained, whether by long-term contract, one-year contract or by option year status, will become the top draft picks of the retaining team. Thus, a team that retains ten players will have made its first ten draft picks and will not enter the next draft until the eleventh round. A team that retains seven players would enter the draft in the eighth round, etc.

7. Every team starts with a maximum of ten long-term players. As a result of trades, the number of long term contracts held by any team may change. However, the number of long-term contract players held by any team at any point in time may never exceed 14. Also, the total number of players held on five-year contracts may never exceed two. The number of four-year contracts may never exceed four. The number of three-year contracts may never exceed six. Finally, every team must carry a minimum of seven long-term contracts at all times.

8. Changes in team ownership do not affect contract status. A new owner taking over an abandoned team is bound by all contract terms.

Note: If you end up with a team that has a bunch of retired, Japanese League and DL players with long-term contracts, the owner will obviously have a reason to think about calling it quits. You may be tempted to write rules that would forgive the $100 buyout provision if an owner abandons his franchise, because you want to encourage a new owner to take over the team. Don't do it. You will only create another reason for the old owner to drop out; he won't feel obligated to keep the roster in good shape and he might even know a friend who will take over the team if the $100 buyout penalty can be waived. If there is a genuine "dog" roster in your league, and you are having trouble finding a new owner because the roster stinks, take up a collection starting with guy(s) who brought the dog team's original owner into your league in the first place and make a gift to the new owner — but do this privately, and don't write it into your league rules. [As a general rule, you should NEVER create any situation where a new owner gets better treatment than the old owner would have received.]

24. Retentions

Our league ☐ will ☐ will not have player retentions each year.

If we will have retentions:

A. Each team may keep up to _____ players. Further explanation if the team's position in the previous season or some other reason allows varying the number of retentions for each team _____

_____

_____

B. There is a requirement to keep at least _____ players per team. Further explanation (if necessary) _____

_____

   C. Retained players must be: ☐ given to ☐ phoned in to ☐ FAXed to ☐ other _____
(name of secretary, commissioner or other responsible person) by _____ (time and date).

   D. Other information required to be given to the person in C. above:
     ☐ salary (if you use the auction method)
     ☐ length of contract
     Other _____

_____

   E. Players may be retained for up to _____ years. Further explanation (if necessary) _____

_____

_____

   F. We will have Toppers' Rights (see page 94) on players ☐ Yes ☐ No. If yes, they are available after _____ years and they can be kept for _____ years.

A. A retained player will have the following salary:

_____

_____

_____

_____

B. Salaries of various acquistions:
   Traded players during the season _____
   Traded player during the off season _____
   Free agent _____
   Minor leaguer acquired during the season _____
   Player brought up from the Reserve list or
      farm system_____
   Player who comes over from the Other League (AL to NL
      or NL to AL) during the season_____
   Other _____

   _____

   _____

A FINAL WORD ON RETENTIONS

Retention rules involve some complex issues and can lead to heated discussions when the rules are unclear. If you have never played this game before, you might like to try one year with the understanding that all players will be released at the end of the first season and then decide on what type of retention rules you want. **Do not, however, start a league with the idea that you will handle the retention question after you get to the end of the first season; each owner will then argue from self-interest facing the unique specifics of his own roster.** Settle the rules when everyone can focus on general concepts rather than specific players. Also, when you amend retention rules, always do it at the beginning of the season, before the draft. It makes no sense to build a team with a given set of retention rules and then find out after the season ends that you won't be allowed to keep the players you had planned on keeping.

LEAGUE ADMINISTRATION

> *"Charlie Finley wouldn't think God would make*
> *a good commissioner."*
> *— Warren Giles*

A wise old priest once told us there are two issues that always cause dissent within any organization: money and hierarchy. We have discussed money previously. **Concerning hierarchy, we have a few suggestions to avoid difficulty:**

1. Don't have a commissioner.

Many leagues get started with one energetic personality doing 90% of the work. In a casual league comprised mainly of beginners, it is not unusual for one individual to function as league secretary, keep track of rosters and position eligibility, do all the stats and standings, and explain the rules (which he probably wrote himself). Oh, yes — and he often serves as treasurer, too. Even in leagues that use a professional stat service, it is common to have one person handling all administrative chores and telling the stat service what to do.

Anyone who invests a huge amount of time and effort in any organization expects a certain amount of deference and payback. In a Rotisserie league, that deference and payback usually means that the hard worker hopes to be appointed czar, although he usually chooses a title like Commissioner. Many leagues acquiesce in such arrangements, simply because it is convenient.

Most of the one-man show leagues develop a disease that we call Commissioner Syndrome. The boss starts out with good intentions, generosity toward his fellow owners and a strong sense of fair play. As the season unfolds, however, little problems arise. Gradually he becomes sensitive about people

101

questioning his rules interpretations; increasingly he explains his decisions with answers like, "Because I said so." The Commissioner often has to make up rules as he goes along; first year leagues always have unforeseen problems arise.

The worst symptom of Commissioner Syndrome occurs only if the disease is allowed to proceed unchecked for several years: the same person (guess who) always wins the league.

There are several steps your league can take to prevent Commissioner Syndrome:

(a) Establish an executive committee or troika(as described in RLBA rules) consisting of your three most trustworthy owners, as described below.

(b) If you have a principal officer such league president, secretary, or (shudder) commissioner, write into the rules that this person has no decision-making authority and may only handle simple administrative responsibilities such as opening envelopes, keeping files and answering the phone when the stat service calls to ask for payment.

(c) Make your rules as clear as possible. This is easier said than done, but generally try to start out with a long list of rules and lengthy explanations. Leave little to the imagination. Write in the answers to a number of "what if" questions. Provide illustrative examples. State the league's intentions wherever possible; don't just write the mechanical procedures to be followed. Say "why" if you think the question is going to be asked. It pays to scan through rules of older leagues, if you can find anyone who will give you copies. Over the years you will find your rules growing to address issues that never came up before.

(d) Segregate duties. The more people you have involved in league administration, the less burden will be placed on any individual and the less reason there will be for anyone to get the idea that he is running the league. The treasurer should be someone other than the secretary who tracks roster moves. Have the secretary report all transactions to the treasurer when he reports fees to be collected. It pays to have two people looking at everything.

2. Be democratic, but don't stop and take a vote every time you have a question.

The only disease worse than Commissioner Syndrome is Chaos Syndrome. Some leagues have no strong personality or anyone willing to make a decision on anything, so they end up meeting once a month (or even more frequently) to discuss all the problems that have arisen since their last meeting and how to deal with them. Frequent meetings are OK, even fun. But voting on rules every few weeks is nuts. Incredibly, some leagues actually vote on questions like position eligibility, DL status and dates, and fees adjustments throughout the summer.

During the course of a baseball season, numerous events are going to occur that never happened before. You won't have a specific rule provision that covers every possibility. But you can't stop and have a legislative session every time something new happens. The best way to handle new questions and little disputes that may arise from time to time is to have an Executive Committee comprised of three owners elected by the league.

Qualifications for Executive Committee candidates are seniority in the league, experience in other leagues, capability to think impartially, knowledge of the rules and financial solvency. The Executive Committee addresses any questions raised by any owner.

In the end, you have to be democratic, so the Executive Committee decisions must be subject to review and approval by the league as a whole, if anyone feels like they just can't live with a particular decision. Everyone should feel confident about this right to make an appeal whenever their conscience tells them to do so, but if you have someone calling for a vote every time the E.C. makes a decision he doesn't like, the guy probably just isn't happy in your league and should be so advised.

On the subject of people dropping out of any league, especially in the middle of a season, we have an unforgiving attitude. Most leagues involve the creation of long-term contracts and retained players, so we generally believe that anyone who makes such commitments should try to hang around long enough to honor them or at least find a responsible replacement in event of contingencies like being sent overseas.

Every league eventually has a quitter, however, and you may as well prepare to deal with that situation before it happens. Our suggestion is a substantial cash deposit for league membership. Pick your own definition of "substantial." We think a number like $1000 or some amount representing about two years of active participation would be about right, but your league might like some higher or lower number. The point is to get people to take their franchise seriously. When an owner leaves in good standing with a smooth transition to a new owner, he gets his deposit back.

Deposits provide a cushion against people quitting with unpaid transaction or stat service fees, and deposits will accumulate interest that can be used for good purposes, such as funding an annual banquet that includes spouses. Think of saying, "Honest, darling, this dinner is free; the league pays for it!"

6TH INNING

THE FOUR ESSENTIALS OF WINNING

> *"As long as I've got one chance to beat you,
> I'm going to take it."*
> — *Leo Durocher*

THE LINEUP

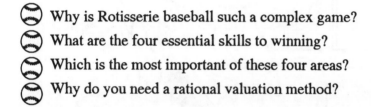

Why is Rotisserie baseball such a complex game?

What are the four essential skills to winning?

Which is the most important of these four areas?

Why do you need a rational valuation method?

Winning Rotisserie baseball is a lot like winning at horse racing, just much more complex. There are hundreds of horses in the field. It takes over six months to run the race and many horses enter or leave the field while the race is in progress. You bet on 23 to 40 horses, not just one. You must bet on specified numbers of certain types of horses. You can move your bets from one horse to another while the race is in progress. If your horse breaks a leg, you can pick another horse, but only after he is officially scratched. At the end of the race, you must parlay some of the bets. And one more detail: your horses are running in four different races, simultaneously, all on the same track.

These complexities of Rotisserie baseball make it difficult for many people to see the big picture. Most writers and analysts have adopted a worm's eye view, not a bird's eye view,

When you are trying to win your league,
you have to focus on all of the essentials of the game;
many writers and owners forget this.

when analyzing Rotisserie baseball. They choose one of two methods to avoid any comprehensive attempt at dealing with the game:

(1) Some see the complexity, and turn away from it entirely. They choose to write about the fun of the game, how to get started, the fascinating twists and turns, and the joy of winning. If they give any advice, it is anecdotal, entertaining, and seldom rigorous. The "fun" subjects — such as what kind of food to have on draft day and how to choose your team logo — have their place in Rotisserie literature. We realize it isn't easy to write about the rules and technical aspects of Rotisserie baseball and its offshoots without being anecdotal and humorous. Having just tried to explain all the rules ourselves, we have an increased respect for the people who tackle these subjects routinely. However, winning is another question, and many writers never get to it.

(2) Some authors seize on one small aspect of the game. Like the blind men touching parts of an elephant in the poem by John Godfrey Saxe, they make valid observations but fail to see the whole beast. Therefore they draw false conclusions. Feeling a leg, they say the elephant is like a tree. Touching his trunk, they think they have found a type of snake. Then one grabs the tusk and says the elephant is a sort of spear. They are all right and all wrong.

VALUATION

The favorite elephant-part for Rotisserie analysts is the question of player valuation: given a set of player stats, what is the dollar value that should be assigned to them? This is an important question that must be addressed somewhere in the subject of winning Rotisserie baseball, but it is hardly the beginning or the end, or even a big part of the middle.

People get hung up on valuation just because it is the one aspect of Rotisserie that separates it from other contests to see who can pick the best players. People play in leagues using

APBA or Pursue the Pennant rules; they pick their players at the start of the season, but they don't have a $260 auction. Other people play simple contests like "let's see who can pick a lineup that hits the most homers this year," and they don't worry about dollar values either. These people would do well at Rotisserie immediately, even if they have never heard of player valuation.

> *"What's all this excitement about baseball again?*
> *I thought they decided who the champions*
> *were last fall."*
> *— Robert Orben*

At the core, Rotisserie is just a game to pick the best players at the start of the season. The way the game works, someone with superior auction skills will have a definite edge over someone who lacks such skills, but the key is knowing your players, not knowing your arithmetic.

For the coming baseball season, which would you rather know . . .

(a) Which rookie pitcher is going to win 19 games with a 2.98 ERA? Or:

(b) What will be the relative scarcity and precise value of a home run, versus a stolen base, in the American League this year?

I hope you said (a). If I had told you, in April 1990, that Cecil Fielder was going to jack 51 home runs, you would have a big advantage over the people who didn't have a clue that such a performance was coming, even if those people knew all about the value of a home run and you didn't.

You would have done just fine in the auction, with little knowledge of player valuation.

> *"There is no such thing as second place.
> Either you're first or you're nothing."*
> — *George Weiss, as Yankee general manager*

HOW TO BE A CHAMPION

If you look at Rotisserie baseball as a year-long game of skill, there are four essentials to winning, and you have to be good at all of them (or very damn lucky) if you want to win your league:

1. **Forecasting player performance.**
2. **Assigning value and rankings based on statistics.**
3. **Conducting the draft or auction.**
4. **Managing your roster after the draft.**

It is intuitively obvious that forecasting is the most important; if you can see the future better than others, you should win. And yet valuation receives more attention than forecasting in many of books and essays about this game.

If you perform poorly in conducting the draft, your work on forecasting and valuation can be undone. You need skills to assemble a good roster during the course of an auction and you mustn't make any blunders on money management. Three bad minutes in a draft or auction can undo three months of preparation. The main issue is simply taking care, however. If you write the wrong address on a letter when you mail it, the work that went into your letter-writing might be wasted. But when you read a book about how to compose a letter, you don't want half of it devoted to address accuracy.

Player valuation simply isn't a complex issue and precision in valuation simply isn't relevant. You can argue for months about the question of whether a player's value is going to be $27 or $29, given a certain performance level, but you're wasting your time with such questions.

Before the auction, you should be thinking about the underlying performance level: How much is this player going to play during the season, where will he appear in the batting order, who is batting in front of him and behind him, what ballpark is he playing in this year and how healthy and consistent he has been in the past. If you know all these things (or at least know as much as you can find out without becoming obsessive in your research), and if you know that his value is likely to be around $28 (plus or minus a buck or two). Stop thinking about that player and start thinking about some other player. Certainly you should be thinking about player performance before the draft, not thinking about whether he will be a little over $28 or a little under $28 this year.

During the auction, you should be watching the other owners, and keeping track of the money, rosters, and available players. If you sit there agonizing about whether you should bid $27 or $29 for the star first baseman Joe Bimbleman, then the whole game is going to pass you by. Try playing poker with a calculator as your main focus, and you will see what we mean.

There are some sophisticated quantitative techniques that can be used to your advantage during an auction, but the complex parts involve questions about your probability of getting a certain player at a certain price, not the question of valuation arithmetic.

In the following chapters, we will review each of the four essentials. **They will be given attention appropriate to their relative importance, which is (roughly):**

Forecasting player performance - 50%
Valuation based on expected stats - 20%
Conducting the draft or auction - 20%
Managing the roster (trades, injuries, etc.) - 10%

You may quibble with our percentages, but you cannot deny the necessity for competence in all four areas.

Without good forecasts, your valuations will be useless. People who came to their 1991 auctions with a precisely elegant ideas about what Carney Lansford had been worth during 1990 didn't find this "information" very useful; what they needed to know was that Carney Lansford didn't have a great outlook for playing time during 1991.

Without a rational valuation method, your forecasts will not always lead to wise draft decisions. For example, if you use some half-baked formula (just for example) that home runs are worth 25 cents apiece, and stolen bases are worth 20 cents apiece, etc., and you value all players accordingly, and you end up with $4000 of calculated value in a ten-team league that has only $260 per team ($2600 total), your values based on $4000 will have you overbidding for every name that comes up. (At least you will fill out your roster quickly and can go home early.)

You have to conduct your draft or auction rationally. You can't win your league if your plan is "pay any price necessary to get Will Clark." Likewise, you can't use your first round pick to draft Randy Velarde, just because he was a friend of yours in school. And there is more to the auction/draft than just being scientific. If you go to an auction and bid up to full, calculated value, without recognizing the independent dynamics of competitive bidding, you will never finish higher than third even if your forecasts and valuations are perfect. In an auction with ten owners, there will be ten different opinions of what each player is worth. From your point of view, every time someone buys a player for a price higher than you had expected, that owner will be wasting some money. Over the course of an auction, a great deal of money gets wasted, meaning that prices must drop (from your point of view) later in the auction, when there is relatively more talent available and less money available, than there was at the beginning of the auction. Understanding this concept and being patient will work wonders for you.

Finally, if you traded your two top stars for a couple of flashy rookie pitchers on April 30, you have probably wasted your scouting, your valuation, and your successful draft.

> *"You may go a long time without winning,*
> *but you never forget that scent."*
> — *Steve Busby, as a Royals pitcher*

Much of what follows in this section is common knowledge, or at least common sense. Much of it has been published before, mainly by us. If it bores you, consider it a checklist, and move quickly to Volume II. If you are a beginner or haven't seen our methods and advice before, then we think you are going to find some valuable lessons in the following pages, and your performance will reflect that fact. Winning isn't everything, but losing is nothing.

7TH INNING

SCOUTING AND FORECASTING

> *"There is one word in America that says it all,*
> *and that one word is, 'You never know.' "*
> — *Joanquin Andujar*

THE LINEUP

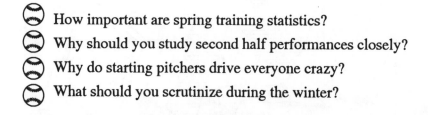

How important are spring training statistics?

Why should you study second half performances closely?

Why do starting pitchers drive everyone crazy?

What should you scrutinize during the winter?

So you have a joined a Rotisserie league, and you want to prepare for draft day. Where do you start? Hopefully, you have enough time to do some meaningful homework. If you just got into this Rotisserie league on Thursday, and your draft is tomorrow, you have a problem. The best you can do is grab some of the spring training annuals at your newsstand and find a book with some projected dollar values for the coming year. If you can't find the Rotisserie Baseball Annual (see page __) at your local bookstore, you might be stuck with one of those books that tells you only what players were worth last year and the year before — not much use, but better than nothing.

The fastest cram course — and many people have been using this last-minute method for several years — is to get this

*It's very comforting to know that you have prepared
well for the upcoming season.*

year's Rotisserie Baseball Annual directly from Devyn Press at 800-274-2221 and look at the forecast stats and $ values for the coming year. It's amazing how many people call on Thursday, or even Friday, before a Saturday draft and order a copy to be shipped Federal Express. Having the book helps you during the draft, but studying it for a couple of weeks or longer is a much better idea.

People who follow baseball during the winter — or at least start watching during spring training — do much better than people who wait until the last minute to start preparing for their draft. There is a natural flow to the distillation of talent, starting during September of the previous season and moving through the instructional leagues, winter ball and up to the last few days of spring training. It is much easier to understand the significance of daily events if you have been following this whole process and have a sense of perspective and direction that each team is taking.

To provide a starting point, we will assume that you are joining a league about two weeks before opening day, near the end of spring training. From that point, you will have time to review a variety of information before draft day. If you start before March 20, so much the better.

SPRING TRAINING: WHO'S PLAYING?

The first thing you want to do in late March is to look at spring training box scores to see who's playing. Using this method, you would have found Cecil Fielder in 1990, even though he wasn't included in ANY of the so-called spring training annuals. You would also have noticed that Cecil had been hitting home runs — three in one game.

We don't pay a lot of attention to spring training performance statistics, except to the extent that they influence management's decision about who makes the team and who doesn't. What we do watch closely is the presence or absence of competition for each position on the field.

Back in spring training 1990, you would have noticed that Cecil Fielder didn't have a lot of competition for the Tigers first base job (the elderly Dave Bergman, maybe?) and that the Tigers didn't have a regular DH, either. That information would have told you that Cecil was likely to play. Looking into his major league track record before he went to Japan in 1989, you would have found that Cecil had 31 HR in 506 at bats for Toronto over parts of three seasons and that he was just a kid when he produced those numbers. We are getting ahead of ourselves, however. The point is that you should look at who's playing during spring training as a starting point for each season.

There are a few cautions to exercise while you are staring at spring training box scores. We have already mentioned that the statistics themselves don't mean much. The only important statistic is playing time. For several years, we kept track of spring training stats and compared them to actual performance during the official season that followed. What we found was:

1. Historically good hitters will usually do well during the official season, regardless what they do during spring training. A poor spring training is not a tip-off that a veteran has faded. If you find a serious injury, that's significant, but a .150 batting average doesn't mean anything. Veterans who have already earned their roles may be experimenting with new batting stances, new methods of guess-hitting or simply enjoying the sun.

2. Historically bad hitters are likely to continue their weak hitting during the regular season, even if they hit .400 during spring training.

3. Hitters with no major league track record (i.e. the rookies) might be able to win a spot on their team's opening day roster with a hot spring training performance, but their stats during the actual season will be consistent with their minor league track record (see Volume 2: *Playing For Blood*) regardless of what happened during spring training. Again, the spring training stats really don't mean anything. It amazes us how some major league teams can make significant roster decisions on the basis of performance during spring training; the games are noncompetitive and the statistical sample is so small as to be near meaningless. Most organizations have years of accumulated stats and scouting reports, etc. It makes no sense to think that three hot weeks in a spring training camp are enough to displace years of evidence. Anyway, you don't have to make the same mistake. Ignore the stats and just look at playing time.

Another point of caution when dealing with spring training box scores is to watch out for trial periods, especially during the early weeks. Most teams will eventually put their "real" opening day lineup on the field, day after day, to tune up for the regular season. During the first three weeks of March, however, you will often see a backup candidate playing the same position every day, while the veteran (who is already assured that he has the starting job) will sit on the bench, pinch hit or occasionally appear out of position. There is no fixed date when these experiments must come to an end. We think you can usually see the real lineup of every team by March 25 each year, but you should get some outside confirmation before concluding that a regular player has been displaced, even if it's two days before opening day and the veteran still hasn't appeared much.

Another caution: try to ignore "split squad" box scores. Split squad games (usually marked "SS" in the newspaper) occur when a team plays two games on the same day. For example, the White Sox may play one game at home against the Pirates in Sarasota and another game versus the Blue Jays in Dunedin at the same time; obviously they must field two teams. Long ago, management might have split the team into an A squad and a B squad, but in recent years it has been common practice to put a few star players in each lineup when a team must split. (Is it possible that somebody actually considers the box office aspect of spring training games?) There are some subtle methods to elicit real information from split squad box scores, such as trying to identify the token stars on an otherwise second-rate squad or looking for efforts to pair upcertain shortstops and second basemen, etc. However, it is better to forget the split squad box scores completely unless you are extremely familiar with a team's roster.

Finally, for those who go to spring training, do not be impressed by one-game performances. Every player in a major league camp is good enough to go 5 for 5 or to pitch six perfect innings on any given day. If you see that day, you will be tempted to think that you have inside information. You don't! You simply saw one professional athlete performing at his peak for one day. Even week-long performances can be visually deceptive as to a player's speed and power. Sometimes, whole major league organizations become deluded about a particular player during spring training.

John B: When I was in St. Petersburg during the last week of March in 1987, Jim Lindeman was playing every day for the Cardinals, smashing torrid line drives every time he swung the bat. And he sparkled in the field, flying through the air for incredible catches, cutting down runners with superhuman throws. The Cardinals saw the same things I saw and concluded that a .251 batting average at Louisville in 1986 was a good enough springboard to the majors, given this terrific month of March. So the Cards traded away Andy Van Slyke and installed Lindeman in right field. He hit .208 and returned to Louisville before the year was over. Yes, he was on my roster, too.

Watching spring training can be a full-time job. I know, because I have done it. You get up in the morning, read papers from Miami, Orlando, Tampa and Fort Myers to get feature coverage of all teams (I haven't yet gone so far as to get Phoenix papers delivered to Florida; maybe this year), and then catch one game in the afternoon and one in the evening. If your vacation plans don't allow room for all this activity, you can always subscribe to Winning Rotisserie Baseball (203-834-0812) or call me during spring training at 900-773-7526.

LAST YEAR'S NUMBERS

Some time before draft day, possibly as early as October if you follow this game year round, you are going to find yourself staring at last year's numbers and studying them intently. Everybody does it. In fact, that's the problem with last year's numbers. Everybody gets them in USA TODAY right after the season ends and everybody looks at them all winter. Some people study last year's numbers excessively. When you get to the point where you find yourself remembering the numbers without having to look them up, we would say you have studied them more than enough.

Our advice is to spend less time looking at last year's numbers. True, you have to start somewhere and last year's numbers are a convenient starting point. We will tell you why they are convenient:

- The calendar year is the official "accounting period" for major league baseball records and championships, etc.
- Last year covers the same length of time that you are now trying to forecast, i.e. one season.
- Existing data are usually sorted and analyzed by year: last year, the year before, two years ago, etc.
- Almost all publications, stats on disk, etc. are focused on last year.
- Your league standings from the previous year are based on the one-year period.

The main problem with last year's numbers is that there is TOO MUCH material focused on them. It is so easy to get your hands on last year's stats, all exquisitely computerized, scrutinized and summarized, that there is an overwhelming temptation to stop after you have seen enough of last year's numbers, because you are fed up with them. After spending 600 hours during the winter reviewing stats to the point of having them almost memorized, you feel justified in calling it quits. You know that you have studied just as hard as anyone else in your league. Isn't that enough? The problem is not that you must study MORE, but that you must study DIFFERENTLY.

We are advising you to spend LESS time studying last year's numbers. They make you blind after a while. Part of the problem is that everyone else in your league will also know last year's numbers, backwards and forwards, because they have been deluged with the same "information" that you have. To win a Rotisserie baseball league, you must have some new ideas, some insight, some different way of looking at the past. When everybody uses the same information exclusively, the game becomes a contest to see who can perform the most rigorous manipulations of last year's numbers. That is not much fun, and even worse, it will make your performance mediocre.

Our advice is to put last year's numbers into a new context, as quickly as possible after you receive them. Keep a historical file on a computer, if you can. Dump the most recent year's numbers in, as soon as you get them, and produce a new "model" of long term performance. A fast and dirty method to put career hitter stats into context, is to weight them, say 50% / 33% / 17% for the past three years, or 50% / 25% / 15% / 10% for the past four years, and create a "weighted average" annual performance.

Another step you can take is to break down last year's numbers into the first half and second half. The next section of this book devotes major attention to the subject of second half numbers. Other publications that aim to educate you about this game are just beginning to see the importance of analyzing second half numbers.

You don't have to wait for John's annual book to start analyzing second half numbers. Save a file of stats at the All Star break, and when you get the full year numbers, just subtract the first half to get the second half. You can begin scrutinizing the second half before the LCS is finished and it will do you more good than scrutinizing those full year numbers that have always caught your attention in October.

120

Need another idea or two? Start looking at players' careers in terms of playing time, not calendar time, especially when younger players are involved. A rookie season of 150 at bats is not the same as a rookie season with 500 at bats. Three or four "years" as a utility player may produce only as much development as one year as a playing regularly. Robert O. Wood invented the method of splitting a veteran players' careers into 10 equal parts, so that every player has a "first decile" equal in significance to every other player's first decile, based on plate appearances rather than days on a roster. You can do the same thing yourself.

If any new activity can simply get your attention away from last year's numbers, it is a worthwhile activity. You can transform last year's numbers into per-at-bat statistics and then make comparisons. You can match last year against two years ago and do a "fluctuation analysis" to see who is most improved and who is fading fastest. You can combine the two methods and compare per-at-bat numbers for the current year versus per-at-bat for the previous year.

Baseball information comes in annual doses and then gets filed away under annual classifications. We can say simply "1969 Mets" or "1988 Dodgers" or "1964 Phillies" or "1986 World Series" and people can immediately visualize specific players and accomplishments. Almost everything significant in baseball gets a year attached to it, and almost every year has its signature personalities. Try free association, either way: 1951? Bobby Thomson. Roger Maris? 1961.

Statistics, in particular, are stated in terms of per-year totals and averages. When you say, "Joe Bimbleman had 25 homers" that means 25 in one year. Almost all of the big questions in baseball are questions about one year: Can Cecil Fielder hit 50 homers again? Will anyone ever hit 60 homers again? Does the team have a 20-game winner? Are there any "40/40" players left in the game today? You don't have to say "per year," because everyone knows that's what you mean.

During any given season, there is a natural tendency for

observers to focus on whatever evidence has become available so far "this year" and to attach undue significance to these partial results, as if they were just as important as any previous annual results. When Scott Erickson was leading the league with a 1.83 ERA half way through 1991, he got just as much attention and respect at that point as he would have earned by posting a 1.83 ERA for a full year. There was no other evidence available to contradict or modify the stated results up to that point in time. Indeed, in mid-1991 many people were looking back at Erickson's 1990 performance and noting the 1.35 ERA during September as confirmation that the new superman was for real. Nobody was saying, "Hey, it's only half a year of great performance . . . he will probably finish the season with an ERA around 3.00." Everyone was inclined to believe that "so far this year" was synonymous with "this year in total."

Early results stick in our memory. Take April for example: we still remember that Graig Nettles once hit 9 HR in April. Ron Cey got 11 jacks in April one year. It was big news at the time. Did you ever hear about how many homers anybody hit during July? Nobody gets national attention for hitting 9 homers during July. By midseason, you would need a dozen HR in a month just to get anyone to lift an eyebrow. If you hit 12 homers in April, people would scream and roll in the aisles and talk about the Hall of Fame.

We get a steady flow of numbers during the season. On April 30 we look at April stats and think about them. On May 31 we look at April-May stats and reflect further. On June 30 we look at April-May-June numbers and on July 31 we look at April-May-June-July. The cumulative effect of all this looking at numbers is that April gets over-emphasized in our thinking. So does May and June.

When do we stop and look at every player's isolated July-August performance? Or August-September? The later months just don't ever get the national population of fans looking at their results, but April-May results get that kind of scrutiny in print and broadcast media, because on May 31 all the stats they have to talk about are April-May stats.

John B.: Several years ago, I took a liking to second half numbers. To some extent I liked them because they were the "underdogs" of the statistical world. They were ignored, overlooked and under-appreciated. Another reason why I liked second half stats was that they gave me an advantage over the people who didn't know about them. Although they are underappreciated, second half stats are potentially more important than first half stats.

I didn't invent the idea of looking at second half numbers. It is an old baseball axiom that a rookie's true value is measured in his second tour around the league, after pitchers have had time to study him. Matt Nokes hit .289 as a rookie, but his performance changed during the season; he hit well over .300 in the first half and .251 in the second half. He has been a .251 hitter ever since.

If you want to win at Rotisserie baseball, you should get used to the idea of studying second half numbers. Many magazines and annuals have started focusing on second half numbers, just as I predicted they would when I started including them in my annual book in January 1989.

Last year's second half numbers are, after all, more recent evidence than the first half numbers that get so much attention. The anecdotal evidence is endless. Just for example: Barry Bonds stole 20 of his 32 bases in the second half of 1989. The 1990 preview book said he could steal 40 bases in 1990 and he stole 50.

Gerald Young stole 65 bases in 1988, but then only 34 in 1989. What was a reasonable expectation for 1990? In John's 1990 annual preview, he noted that Young stole only three bases in the second half of 1989, while getting caught nine times. We concluded that something was wrong and warned you off. Young stole six bases in 1990. People who went into 1990 expecting him to steal 40 to 50 bases (his average in 1988-1989) are now scrutinizing second half stats.

Neal Heaton began throwing a forkball in the July 1989. In the second half of '89, his ERA was 1.66 and his BPI ratio was 1.03. But no one noticed the extent of Heaton's turnaround, because his full year numbers kept reflecting the horrible first half that had motivated him to experiment. The conventional media didn't start asking what had happened until early 1990, when Heaton was still getting everyone out. In early 1900, Heaton was suddenly leading the National League in ERA. It amused us to hear all the conventional media people asking Heaton, "What are you doing different THIS YEAR?" By looking at second half stats, we knew that Heaton had started doing something different in mid-1989. Like all pitchers, he finally went sour again, but the point is that it took most observers about nine months to realize when Heaton had reached his peak.

Todd Worrell lost his physical abilities in the second half of 1989. He had a 5.09 ERA in the second half. But the people focused on "last year" knew only that Worrell had a 2.96 ERA that year. The people who drafted Worrell in 1990 ruined their Rotisserie rosters; they all blamed bad luck, but they should have blamed bad homework.

The anecdotal evidence goes on and on. You can find many more stories like the above in the annual Rotisserie Baseball Analysts. But the point is already clear: **second half stats are surely worth a long, hard look, as PART of your annual effort to forecast player performance for the coming year.**

Why is the second half so important?

(1) The second half of the preceding year is chronologically close to the period that we are trying to predict. Events that occurred early in the preceding year (like Todd Worrell's 1.21 ERA in the first half of 1989) are less relevant than events that occurred late in the preceding year (like Todd Worrell's 5.00 ERA in the second half of 1989) because the older events are chronologically more remote.

In a baseball forecasting context, events that happened

ten years ago are meaningless. A two-year-old event is possibly meaningful, but is still suspect because of its age. Events just one year old are more relevant than two-year-old events and things that happened late last year are usually more meaningful than those that happened early last year. Second half stats give us a picture, a valuable little snapshot, in which the more remote events of the previous year (i.e. April, May and June) have been eliminated.

(2) **IF SOMETHING HAPPENED during the preceding year that changed a player's abilities and output, that "something" will be more heavily reflected in the second half numbers than in the full year numbers.** If whatever it was that happened occurred on July 4th, that event will be fully reflected in second half statistics, 50% reflected in full year statistics and not-at-all reflected in first half statistics of the preceding year.

Some events get into the news and some don't. You could have researched Worrell's injury in 1989. If you lived in Pittsburgh you might have had a clue that Neal Heaton developed a new pitch in July 1989. But many changes are not publicized and many are difficult to investigate.

As we all know, things can happen during the long baseball season. A hitter may be moved in the batting order. The players batting in front of him or behind him in the batting order may change. The player's team may be changed. Opposing defenses may be relocated to a hitter's disadvantage or his own fielding position may be shifted and have an adverse or favorable effect on his hitting. All these factors affect statistics even when a player's innate skills, attitude, concentration and total playing time remain exactly the same.

(3) **Skills can change, too.** A young hitter may learn (finally!) to lay off the high fastball or to go the other way with an outside pitch. He may learn such things gradually over the course of several years, he may learn them during one season or he may learn them suddenly on July 4th. An

older hitter may lose some speed and get to first base on time less often, or he may lose his ability to get around on a fastball. Or pitchers may simply LEARN that the old man can no longer jerk their fastball into the seats. Word spreads fast among pitchers around a league.

(4) Rookies, not veterans, are most susceptible to opposing pitchers and managers learning something that is going to impair their hitting performance. As noted above, the cornerstone of the "second half theory" is the old baseball axiom that a rookie's true ability can be seen in his second tour around the league.

John B.: In January 1989 I began publishing details of second half numbers, even $ values based on second half performance, and the response has been overwhelming. Even though I didn't invent second half analysis (that baseball axiom about rookies is at least ninety years old) I am proud to be the first person who pursued this idea extensively in print for Rotisserie and forecasting purposes.

My enthusiasm for second half numbers has been such that many people (who should know better) have suggested that second half stats are the sole basis for my forecasts and predictions. It is flattering to have people think "Benson's idea" whenever they hear about second half scrutiny, but it is obviously silly to turn that association around backwards and say "second half stats method" whenever they hear someone say "Benson forecast." When a Yankee coach told me, in September 1990, that Matt Nokes was likely to displace Bob Geren as the regular catcher in 1991, I didn't use a calculator to figure that Nokes would have a good year in 1991, while Geren's value would plummet.

Quoting from the first three editions of the Rotisserie Baseball Annual: "Second half annualization is definitely useful, but it is just one tool available. When you finally make a determination and put your money where your mouth is, you should have considered numerous factors and various points of view, not just second half performance."

Forecasting is not a mathematical exercise. There is no such thing as a "mechanical forecast" except in the world of people who don't know what they are doing. You may start a forecast process with a mechanical projection, but that is the beginning of the forecast, not the end. Our method is to individually scrutinize each player, using original information directly from players, coaches and managers wherever possible. Within the part that is purely analytical, second half stats are just one more place where people should look for clues. We stress the importance of looking, because so many people don't look and they don't see.

Drafting players for Rotisserie purposes is a lot like hiring people for professional positions. In hiring, there are several steps that should be followed. You should look at credentials. You should interview. You should check references. You should give a pre-employment physical exam. But when somebody says, "That manager hires his people on the basis of physical exams," they are showing their ignorance of the total process.

So keep things in perspective and you will find all kinds of nuggets that give you an edge in Rotisserie competition. When you like players for numerous reasons (the right age, the right ballpark and a good second half in the previous season) then you are on the right track. The forecast stats in the annual Rotisserie Baseball Annual are John's first complete and "official" forecast for the coming year. An updated forecast appears in the April issue of the Winning Rotisserie Baseball monthly. Tables of second half stats from the preceding year are presented for your reference and enjoyment. They are worth studying, but they are not forecasts, projections or anything if taken out of context.

INTRODUCTION TO FORECASTING:

ROTISSERIE RECOMMENDATION:
THINK "CONTEXT!"

If you get one lesson from this book, let it be this: put all numbers and ideas into context, and you will play this game better.

If you see some fact or number that catches your eye — take a superstar performance in Winter Ball for example — put that piece of information into context. Is the person involved on a major league roster? Has he ever before done anything similar in baseball? Does he have a good chance to play, or is he waiting in line behind Roberto Alomar or Will Clark, with no chance of being traded? If he does get to play, will he bat leadoff or clean-up like he did in Puerto Rico this winter, or will he bat ninth and be used only occasionally against lefty pitchers? Summary: think CONTEXT.

There are four types of people who play Rotisserie baseball: (1) those who are good and know it, (2) those who are good but underrate their own abilities, (3) those who are weak/novices and know it, and (4) the most dangerous group to deal with — those who think they know what they are doing when they don't.

Some readers who fall into this fourth category will have problems as a result of reading this book, because they will take things out of context. They will reveal their narrow-minded approach by drawing false inferences based on over-generalization. For example, they will say, "Benson uses second half stats to forecast performance for the coming year. Bimbleman had a good second half, so Benson must like him." Or: "Benson uses a player's age to forecast improvement. Bimbleman is age 26 this year, so Benson must like him." You get the idea. If you hear anybody making general statements that indicate a lack of perspective and a tendency to take ideas out of context, get them into your league, because they make excellent, also-rans.

The single most important context is one that you must describe for yourself: the strength of your own Rotisserie league and your competitive situation within that league.

128

One of the most popular pre-draft questions from people who call 1-900-773-7526 is: "Who's a good sleeper?" That's a difficult question to answer, for someone who is not familiar with what your competitors know and what they don't know.

In March 1989, we often recommended Joe Boever as a "sleeper." At that time, he had only one major league save, but John had been watching him for two years in the Cardinals organization (stuck behind Todd Worrell) and could see that he had great stuff (at that time) and the mentality to be a closer. We also saw that the Braves bullpen was short of talent and we noted that Boever had performed brilliantly in 20 innings of work in late 1988.

It was amusing to note the variety of reactions when we gave Boever's name as a sleeper. Some said, "Oh, everybody knows about Boever. He's obvious; I need someone obscure." Other people said: "Joe who? What team is he on?" This diversity was further evidenced in actual Rotisserie auctions in April 1989. Boever sold for only $1 to $3 in a third of all auctions and yet he sold for prices of $20 or higher in almost a third of all auctions as well. It was obvious what happened: In many leagues, two or more people visualized a source of 20+ saves and the price soared. In numerous other leagues, only one bidder (or nobody) attached much value to Boever and his price stayed very low.

So the context of your league could make a player worth $2 or $20 on any given draft day, depending on what people know (or what they think they know). To do well in your league, you really have to assess the competitive situation accurately. From reading this book, you cannot possibly find out what your competitors know or don't know. You must do that competitive intelligence work on your own. So study your competition, and think "context."

THE PROBLEM WITH STARTING PITCHERS

Starting pitchers are the most unreliable, unpredict-

able, unpleasant group of people in the world, statistically speaking that is. Even within a major league team, they are a sub-group unto themselves. They have their own habits and unique superstitions. Starting pitchers generally don't like to talk with media people on the day they are scheduled to pitch; some of them won't even talk to their own teammates, for fear of damaging their concentration. How many hitters are so careful about preparing for a game?

Pitchers are not crazy to put so much emphasis on concentration. There is something about the art of pitching that causes a tiny shift in performance to produce a tremendous difference in measured results. The same pitcher might win 18 games one year and just 8 the next. A pitcher with an "established" career ERA of 3.50 is always capable of producing an ERA as low as 2.50 or as high as 4.50 in any given season. It happens all the time. These big changes in stats can occur with no observable change in physical abilities. When a pitcher actually experiences a change, such as learning a new pitch, or losing some velocity due to injury, you can see him soar to stardom or disappear from the major leagues completely in a very short time.

One of the most complex problems faced by Rotisserians and major league executives alike, is the scouting of talent for starting pitcher roles. Although the problem is complex, we don't recommend that you spend a great deal of time on it. During the winter and spring training, your time would be better spent on other questions.

The best approach to starting pitchers is simple: Just make a list of "OK" candidates, go to the draft or auction looking for bargains and hope for good luck during the season. You can reach the point of diminishing returns very quickly when you scrutinize starting pitchers. Consider the "Cy Young curse" as a starting point: the very best starting pitcher from the previous season is often not a good selection in the next season.

Hitters are much more predictable. Statistically, they usually perform within a predictable range. Variations of

more than 10% or 15%, compared to historic averages, are uncommon in most of the stat categories. A career .250 hitter might hit .225 or .275, but not likely outside that range. Someone who has produced an average of 75 RBI per year might rise or fall by 15 RBI, but he will usually hit in the range of 60 to 90, by just staying healthy and active.

Think about the difference between a good hitter and a bad hitter. A good hitter hits around .300 or better (or say .290 if it makes you happier — the lower the number, the stronger the conclusion that we are building, but it really makes no difference). A bad hitter hits .215 (the actual Mendoza Line — you could look it up). Would you say then, that a "bad" hitter is 215/300 or 72% as good as a "good" hitter? If you think .285 is a good average, then Mario Mendoza is more than 72% as good as a good hitter.

The bad hitter (.215 average) makes an out 78.5 % of the time. A good hitter (.300 average) makes an out 70.0 % of the time. Only 8.5% of the time does a good hitter get a hit when a bad hitter would make an out. The .215 hitter and the .300 hitter do the "same thing" statistically (either both make an out or both get a hit) 91.5 % of the time. You could argue that a bad hitter, based on batting average, is 91% as good as a good hitter; while a bad pitcher is only half as good as a bad pitcher, based on earned run average.

You may quibble with the percentages and stat categories. The above numbers are not intended to be rigorous mathematics. They are intended only to make the point: **there is a big, big difference in stats between the best and worst pitchers in baseball, much more variation than you find among hitters. And the same pitcher can produce big variations from year to year. That point is a cornerstone of common sense when you play Rotisserie. Pitcher performance just isn't predictable within a useful, reliable range.**

Does a pitcher's actual performance — the way he throws the ball, and in what sequence or situation — change that much from year to year? We don't believe it can because active major league pitchers are all at the highest level in a large pyramid of talent. If there are, about 300 pitchers (the major league rosters plus the disabled list, etc.) in major league ball at any given moment, that is 300 people out of about 100 million males between the ages of 18 and 40 in the U.S., Canada, and Central American / Caribbean area. How good are those 300? All of them are absolutely excellent! How big is the real skill difference between the best and the worst among those 300? Pretty darn small.

Conclusion? The stats we use to measure pitchers, especially ERA and wins, tend to grossly magnify and exaggerate the real differences in quality of performance. On any given day, a tiny factor like a skinned knuckle, a hangnail, a sore toe, or a mental problem like bank account or spouse worries — or a pesky reporter who asked an irritating question — can have a huge and visible impact on a pitcher's observable performance, while the same factors in a hitter's life could be completely invisible for a week or longer. Did the pitcher really throw much different when he had a bad day? Not possible. If his motion or pitch selection really looked that bad, the pitching coach and manager would notice right away, and make a change. Very seldom can the best observers in the universe detect ANYTHING visible until it is too late and by then the stats are cast.

What do you do about it? When you do your scouting and forecasting, spend less time and effort on starting pitchers. Follow a few simple rules. **Look for tall, healthy, hard-throwing lefties who pitch for winning teams in huge ballparks. You can't have all these criteria every time you choose a pitcher, but you can try to get as many as possible crammed into each selection.**

We have more advice about starting pitchers in the chapters covering draft day and roster management, but you start on the right path by allocating your scouting and forecasting time wisely. Struggling to identify the fifth starter on each team is NOT a worthwhile use of time. The person you end up identifying is probably going to have negative value anyway; he will likely be near the bottom of those 300 pitchers in the big leagues. Spend your precious time thinking about the fourth and fifth outfielders and identifying the likely DH against righty pitching on every team. These hitters are roster assets; they won't hurt you, and they will often rise in value (predictably) during the season.

SCOUTING FOR SAVES

While you should save time by not scouting the starting pitchers too extensively, you must put some solid effort into your examination of bullpens. Saves are a critical category in every Rotisserie league. For a good bullpen, you need to know all the proven ace relievers whose teams will not change their stopper role. After the established closers and co-closers, look for hard-throwers who have setup and support roles, especially on teams with unsettled bullpen situations. Veterans with a track record of success in a setup role will usually be favored over talented newcomers, although you should make an effort to know every pitcher who will be competing for those precious saves.

The game's top analysts have repeatedly proven that successful performance in the saves category correlates very highly with victory in Rotisserie baseball. Mike Dalecki, for example, has made annual examinations of a large population of leagues, using regression analysis and correlation coefficients to check which categories are the key to victory. Every year, we publish his results in the Winning Rotisserie Baseball monthly, and every year, the importance of saves is revalidated.

All of the above advice applies to your search for saves: look at long-term track records, last year and second-half stats, and September box scores. During the winter, look for overlaps and vacancies. Roster analysis is especially important when you are looking for saves. An average major league team will win 81 games, and about half of those victories will produce a save. So there are only about 40 saves to go around on each pitching

133

roster. That number won't change much because of the talent in the bullpen.

A major league team can increase its home run output by filling the lineup with sluggers. But talent won't have much impact on the total number of saves. (Note that a bad closer gets a save in about 75% of his save situations; a good closer gets about 85%, not much difference.) In 1991, you could have put Dennis Eckersley, John Franco, Rick Aguilera, Bryan Harvey and Rob Dibble all on the same major league roster, and you still couldn't have gotten more than about 55 saves in total; it just isn't mathematically possible. You have to look at the competition within each roster, not just the track records of the candidates to get saves.

The numbers game can work to your advantage, too. Even the worst major league wins about 60 games every year, meaning that about 30 saves will be recorded by the bullpen on that team. Finding the best reliever on a bad staff can add 20 saves to your team stats. Bullpens always produce value, even on teams that don't have even one starter worth considering.

Searching for saves is complicated by the fact that one of your most important tools — examination of spring training box scores — is not very useful. How can you find saves during spring training? Saves are very scarce to begin with. If a pitcher gets one save a week, that's 26 over the course of a season, so one save per week is a very high output. During spring training, the true ace reliever might get only one or two saves, while a marginal reliever might get lucky and record three or four saves. You can't define roles by looking at the spring save statistic.

One spring training stat that we like to scrutinize is Games Finished (GF). Looking at a box score and seeing an established ace reliever working the ninth inning (and only the ninth inning) gives you a definite indication that the team views him as a closer, no matter what the score was in that game. The team is treating him like an ace reliever, meaning that management discretion is working in his favor. The GF column tells us a great deal about what the manager and the front office are thinking.

Aside from the GF stats, you can look for any pitcher being used for exactly one inning per outing during spring training. Starting pitchers can be spotted because they work three innings, then four, five, or six. The candidates to get saves will almost always be used one inning at a time or maybe two at the most.

The "who's going to play" part of the question is worth considering carefully while you are looking for save artists during the pre-season, despite all these difficulties. In late March, most teams are fielding the same lineups that they plan to use during the regular season. Even when a manager parades out a hoard of pitchers, his starter is usually a "real" starter, and his closer is usually someone who will be given the ball to finish games in July and August.

STAYING IN SHAPE DURING THE WINTER

"It's not the winters that bother me. It's the summers."
— *Walter Alston*

For year-round baseball fans and analytical types, the off-season presents a marvelous opportunity. The numbers finally stop changing long enough to allow some in-depth analysis beyond anything that would be practical during the summer, when new numbers keep spewing out every day. Here are some ideas to get a head start on "next year" any time after last year ends. Remember, as we keep saying, your ultimate goal is to come up with a forecast for the coming season: who is going to play, and how well are they going to do?

The broadcast media generally turn their attention away from baseball during the winter, but the specialized print media follow baseball year round. USA TODAY Baseball Weekly has joined the reliable veteran, The Sporting News, in providing in-depth coverage during the off-season. And Baseball America is especially strong on coverage of minor leaguers and rookies. We recommend getting all three by subscription. You can find them at any good newsstand, but having a complete library will pay off at times. John's own monthly, Winning Rotisserie Baseball, is promoted extensively in this book, because it helps you.

The timeliest annual that shows full career stats for all players, including the season just completed, is the STATS™ Major League Handbook (1-800-63-STATS). They also publish the STATS™ Minor League Handbook, the best review of all minor league players. Both books are available each year in November, which is amazingly early. For more on the annual books worth buying, see Chapter 10.

If you suffer baseball withdrawal during the winter, and find that printed matter just isn't enough to get you through until spring training, you can always look for winter baseball on the Spanish-language cable TV stations. The winter ball playoffs usually get onto one of the cable sports stations. As a last resort, you can always pull out a videotape of a game from the previous season. For scouting purposes, we like to tape at least one game of every team playing against a righty starter and a lefty starter, every year. For fun, you can tape a game without watching it and pull it out on cold winter evening for some out-of-season viewing.

PAYING ATTENTION TO WINTER LEAGUES

Like any short record of baseball statistics, 170 at bats in winter ball can be misleading. Winter ball stats, assuming that a player has been a regular throughout the winter season, are no more significant than the major league stats that you see around May 20 each year. Some of the high-flyers will fall back to earth, and some of the slow-starters will come on strong. Combine the statistical insignificance with the fact that winter ball games are not the most serious competition in the world, or the highest level of play, and you could make a strong argument that the numbers aren't worth any more than a passing glance.

However, if you think again about the major league stats and standings that you see in mid-May, you realize that there are some valuable clues about who is doing better or worse than they did the year before. After 170 at bats, you can often see who is going to be successful among the rookie crop, which veterans are in danger of losing their jobs, and which pitchers are getting powerful results from those new pitches they have been developing.

Winter ball stats give similar clues. You get indications and hints which, in combination with other information that you have accumulated, may lead you to make some accurate assessments and come up with some valuable insights. To give you a feeling for the kind of insights that you can get from winter ball numbers, here are some of the cases that emerged in the past few years.

Lonnie Smith's 1989 comeback, after being released by the Royals, hitting just .237 for the Braves and spending most of the year at Richmond, was heralded by an outstanding winter ball performance. At San Juan in the Puerto Rican League, Smith produced a .366 average, 7 homers, 42 RBI, and 28 stolen bases in just 191 at bats. Combined with the knowledge that Atlanta was short of righty-hitting outfielders, we felt confident that he would get plenty of playing time. Smith's comeback was one of our better predictions that year.

As noted previously in the comments concerning context, one of our readers in 1989 said, "Everybody knew about Joe Boever." By draft day, that was true in many leagues — especially those where people were watching winter stats. Boever was 2-0 with 20 saves (a new P.R. League record), a 2.02 ERA, and 1.02 BPI ratio the winter before he emerged to give the Braves 21 saves. We almost wished he hadn't done so well in winter ball, because we spotted him a full year and a half before 1989. And we certainly wish he hadn't attracted so much attention during spring training. Half of being right is being right about things that other people don't anticipate.

The year before Smith made his comeback and Boever emerged for his one good year as a closer, Caracas had a pitcher named Mike Schooler, the Seattle bullpen prospect. Schooler led the Venezuela league in ERA with 0.59, and produced a ratio of

0.81. The track record before that performance ended with a 3.96 ERA at Chattanooga. For a very low price, some astute Rotisserie owners got 78 saves over the next three years.

The same winter that Schooler had those good numbers, young Greg Maddux went to Venezuela and produced a 7-4 record for last place Zulia, with an ERA of 1.49 and a ratio of 1.07 in 96 innings. Maddux had struggled through a 6-14 season with a 5.61 ERA for the Cubs the year before. Do you think he was a good starter for a price of $1 or $2 that April? Maddux, of course, went 18-8 with a 3.18 ERA for the Cubbies after that winter performance.

Doug Jones reached age 30 with only nine major league saves in ten years as a pro. Then one winter, the soft-throwing Jones led the Puerto Rican League with an 0.51 ERA and a ratio under 0.91, with a strikeout/walk ratio of better than 3:1. All Jones did was get 37 saves for Cleveland during the regular season, and then 32 the next year, and 43 the year after that, with ERA's of 2.27, 2.34, and 2.56.

When Roberto Alomar was a 19-year-old middle infield prospect who had never appeared in the major leagues, he hit .302 with 31 runs scored in 199 AB's. He went on to have a very successful rookie season.

Jose Rijo had a reputation as a wild man (meaning poor control of the strike zone) until he produced an ERA of 1.81 and a ratio of 0.88 in the Dominican league, while walking only 11 in 55 innings. The year before, he had been demoted to the minor leagues after walking 100 batters for the Oakland A's. After that winter performance, Rijo not only returned to the major leagues; he also produced a 13-8 record with a 2.39 ERA and a 1.12 ratio. The walks were never again much of a problem.

The anecdotal evidence goes on and on. Among the young stars who put up huge numbers in winter before delivering good rookie seasons have been Carlos Baerga, Edgar Martinez, Ramon Martinez, Lenny Harris, Greg Vaughn, and many others. **There are two cautions concerning winter ball stats, however.**

(1) Winter ball performances are just one indicator.

There has to be a job opening on the major league roster, before any player can accomplish anything. You can use winter ball stats to confirm what you already believe, but you aren't likely to get any wholly new ideas by following the winter leagues. I liked Joe Boever, Edgar Martinez, Roberto Alomar and many others as major league prospects, long before they had their good winter numbers. The outstanding performances just enhanced my interest. As we keep telling you, think context before reaching any conclusions.

(2) Pitchers who work hard in winter ball have a strong tendency to weaken in August of the following season. They simply get tired. If you end up with a successful acquisition based on winter league performance, consider trading them in late July.

SEEING THE FUTURE

During the winter, you can do a great deal of work for next year by keeping track of changes. Winter meetings, since the end of the collusion era, usually produce a flurry of activity every year, with trades and free agent signings (and some talented free agents going unsigned or leaving for Japan). In October, if you have time to start that early, write down a list of who was playing each position on every team at the end of the previous season, and keep this list up-to-date as players come and go during the winter. You may, of course, rely on other people to do this for you, but you will never marshal any marvelous insights while reading other people's analyses. Starting with raw data lets you develop your own unique perspective.

You can put your lists on a computer, or just scribble them on a piece of paper; for several years we have been using magnetic tags on a visual board, to make sure no player gets lost in the shuffle. Whatever method you use, you will be amazed to see the gaping holes and excess/overlaps that occur during the winter. You can be sure that major league GM's are looking at the same information, and you can often foresee their roster moves long before anything gets into the news.

One of the biggest problems with scouting and forecasting is that the people who make roster decisions in major league baseball often change their minds, or don't have a clear vision of the future in the first place.

Things change. If you had asked the New York Yankees front office on December 30, 1990 to name their five starting pitchers, they would probably have told you that Chuck Cary and Dave Eiland were the two most assured of starting roles, while Tim Leary, Andy Hawkins, Dave LaPoint, and Greg Cadaret would contend for the remaining three jobs. They further would have told you that rehab projects Pascual Perez and Mike Witt were good possibilities, and that Steve Adkins and Kevin Mmahat were the top rookie contenders. If you don't associate these names with Yankee pitching in 1991, there is a good reason: most of the "top ten" candidates on the depth chart didn't figure prominently in the starting rotation. Scott Sanderson arrived as a free agent to become the top starter, and rookies Jeff Johnson, Scott Kamieniecki, and Wade Taylor all won full time starting roles. Four of the five starters weren't even on the list of candidates.

Another classic example came from Atlanta in 1990. On Opening Day, the National League rookie of the year, Dave Justice, was nowhere in sight. The Braves' everyday first baseman was Nick Esasky. After Esasky, the top backups were Tommy Gregg as a left-handed hitter and Francisco Cabrera as a right-handed hitter. Justice was playing outfield in Richmond, while stars like Dale Murphy, Ron Gant, Lonnie Smith and Oddibe McDowell were taking all the outfield time in Atlanta. No one had Dave Justice on their "top rookie" list, not even us. We had taken a long, hard look at him and concluded that there just wasn't room for him in Atlanta that year, despite the obvious power and speed.

Two things changed for the Braves in 1990. Esasky became disabled, creating some time at 1B for Justice, who was called up May 16. Then Dale Murphy was traded on August 4, creating a

140

full time vacancy in right field. In just one third of a season after taking the right field job, Justice produced 20 homers. He finished the year hitting .282 with 28 HR, all unforeseeable in early May.

Nobody in the Rotisserie world bought Dave Justice on draft day, 1990, because he wasn't in the major leagues, and wasn't eligible. In leagues with farm systems, some lucky owners found that farmhand Justice suddenly soared in value; we call them lucky rather than smart, because Justice didn't have a clear path of advancement in the Braves organization. He might still be in the minor leagues today, if it hadn't been for a Esasky's enigmatic case of vertigo and the trade of a franchise player in Murphy. The people who benefitted from Justice during 1990 and deserved credit for clever management were those who grabbed Justice shortly after he reached the majors. The potential was visible to those who looked hard enough.

Given the numerous variables and uncertainties, no one expects you to assemble a Rotisserie team full of players who will all hold their value or get better. On a 23-man roster you are going to have a couple of disappointments; it's part of the game. Your job in managing a Rotisserie team is simply to do the best you can. For dealing with the question, "who's going to play?" your best tactic is just to do your homework.

Even beginners should prepare for draft day by writing down their expectations about who has the starting job on each team at each position (At this point you find one more reason to pick either the AL or NL, not both: you can cut in half the number of players and positions that need watching.) It's OK to start with one of the spring training preview magazines or (better yet) a publication like USA TODAY Baseball Weekly that attempts to project starters for you. Don't stop with a published list, however. Do some kind of research on your own, such as checking box scores to verify what you have read. And stay current on trades and injuries. By writing your own list instead of using someone else's, you at least accept responsibility for the thought process, and you might very well come up with a good idea or two just by going through the motions of thinking.

To compete in any serious league, you will want to make depth charts, not just lists of starting lineups. The more thoroughly you answer the question "what if . . . ?" the better you will do in any league. Usually it's not too hard to see who plays a backup role at each position. From last year's records, you can see who got the call when the regular was hurt or resting. From spring training box scores, you can see who else is being considered and tested by management. Minor leaguers often enter into the picture. Managers often help you out by telling, during spring training, who is the starter and who is next in line at each position. It pays to do your homework.

As you get near draft day, your primary objective is identifying the players who have starting jobs on Opening Day. If your draft day is the first weekend after the major league season starts, you will only have to look at few box scores to see who is playing. The harder part, and the key to victory over the course of a long season, is to find some of the lesser role-players who have good chances to emerge with increased playing time during the season. **The $1 players and the last-round picks who end up having decent seasons are the primary difference between winners and losers.**

The factors to watch are players' ages, abilities, track records facing right-handed and left-handed pitching, durability / injury history, and personal preferences of the manager and general manager who control the team. During your search and review of starting players, you will find some starters who aren't quite as secure as their peers on other teams. Older players, those who are injury-prone, those who have been platooned in the recent past, and players who have found their way into the manager's doghouse are all logical candidates to give up some of their playing time during the year ahead.

When you look at the backup players during your "what if" reviews, you will find the same names filling the contingency slot at multiple positions. For example, a young good-hitting utility infielder has at least four clear chances to win a big increase in playing time. The second baseman, third baseman, or shortstop could get hurt or traded. Any of them might slump badly. And the utility man himself might hit .330 as an occasional substitute, attracting more attention and winning greater consideration as a regular.

When you start doing your homework, you will find numerous study aides. One of your first problems will be separating the wheat from the chaff among all the materials that purportedly are there to help you. There is a great deal of chaff out there and there always will be. We have already recommended several reliable publications. Chapter 10 gives a more complete list of those that have proven helpful and appear most promising in the early 1990's.

We have made some general suggestions on how to spend your time during the winter. If you have a draft in two weeks, not all of these are going to be applicable this year. But if you are getting started in, say, December or January, most of them will apply, and all will be useful sometime during the next year.

There is no such thing as too much preparation for your draft. There are some unproductive ways to spend your time, however, such as over-scrutinizing starting pitchers as we have mentioned. We will leave the subject of scouting and forecasting with one further caution:

ROTISSERIE RECOMMENDATION:
DON'T BET THE RANCH ON ROOKIES

Unless you have a two-year plan to become gradually competitive with a weak, new franchise in an ongoing league, you don't want a roster full of rookies. The hype is overwhelming and drives up perceived values beyond any reasonable amount. Baseball card dealers, major league scouts, fans returning from spring training, team media offices, and everybody you can think of, keep introducing "the next Ted Williams" and "the next Tom Seaver" every year as an annual ritual. Don't listen to them.

Rookies are like lottery tickets. If you get one and win, it's great. But you should approach them as entertainment, not investments. Another parallel with lotteries: people who get lucky will go around telling everyone they know, incessantly; the people who waste their money time after time just don't talk about it. The vast majority of rookies do not live up to expectations.

Even if you know for a fact that a rookie has the potential to hit 20 homers and steal 20 bases, you can't win if you go out and pay the going rate for a 20/20 hitter. The best you can do is get what you pay for, and break even. That's not how to win a Rotisserie league. You need to buy players for less than they're worth ... and if you ever pay up to full value, you want a proven veteran, not an untested kid. Everyone talks about rookies in terms of potential. Even when the prognosticators are right about the talent, it may take two or three years for a talented youngster to reach his potential.

In the draft/auction chapter, we have some suggestions on how you can benefit from rookie hype. The basic idea is to get the other guy all excited about rookies, and let him suffer with them. Everybody wants Jose Canseco, and everybody ends up with Jose Gonzalez. This is one bandwagon you don't to ride on.

8TH INNING

PLAYER VALUATION: KEY ISSUES

> *"They say you have to be good to be lucky, but I think you have to be lucky to be good."*
> — *Rico Carty*

THE LINEUP

- What is the best valuation method to use?
- How much of your $260 should you spend for pitchers in an auction?
- Should you have separate budgets for pitchers and hitters?
- Why does position scarcity affect player valuation?

So you have a list of players. And you have answered the questions (as best you can): who is going to play, and how well are they going to do? You have written down, or obtained, a list of expected stats for every player available in your draft.

Now you are ready to assign rankings and dollar values. Even if you have a simple draft, we recommend that you use dollar values to do your rankings at each position, because you will get a list that says not only who's better, but how much better they are than the next player on your list; this information will be valuable at times during the draft.

If you want to see actual "formulas" and calculation examples, we have put them in Volume II. There isn't any higher mathematics involved here; it's all addition, subtraction, multi-

You have only $260 to spend so you need to budget it wisely.

plication, and division. Anyone is capable of following the arithmetic, or doing it themselves. But we believe that beginning/intermediate players are not likely to be do-it-yourself valuation enthusiasts. And there are numerous printed sources of valuation lists for every player, including especially the forecasts that appear every year in The Rotisserie Baseball Annual, and the update that appears just before draft day in Winning Rotisserie Baseball monthly. If you are not going to do your own value calculations, put some thought into choosing a good source when you obtain them. (See Chapter 10 for a longer list of sources.) If you do want to perform your own value calculations, see Volume II for our recommended method.

There is no "right" valuation method. You just need a rational method that works in your league, and you know your league better than anyone else does. One of the first tip-offs to people who don't know what they're talking about is the claim, "My method is right!" Our recommendation is that you put some energy into choosing a source of dollar values. We hope you will choose the "Benson method" and buy our annual lists, but the main point is to use any source or method that makes you feel comfortable going into your draft or auction. The advice in this chapter will help you see who knows what they're doing, and who doesn't, when it comes to valuation methods.

The valuation problem isn't really very complicated, although people have written whole books about it. You have $260 per team in standard Rotisserie rules. In the old ten-team National League, that's $2600 total. We will use the ten team league as an example throughout this chapter, because it makes much of the arithmetic easier. If you are valuing players in a 12-team league, you will have $3120 to account for ($260 X 12).

Whatever method you use, there are certain checks and balances that must be included. We have given you a complete list of these tests for reasonableness, to help you evaluate the valuation methods. Any method that passes all of these tests will yield essentially the same answers; the only significant differences in values will result from differences in the stats that are forecast for each player.

Before giving you our general guidelines for rational valuation, we have some broad comments about the valuation process itself. One of the biggest problems that you will encounter when you deal with valuation, whether you simply pick up a printed list, follow someone else's recipe, or do everything yourself on a computer, is that most people jump into the valuation arithmetic without stopping to think about what they are doing and why. The danger in going straight to the arithmetic is that you create an illusion that your results are "answers" and that you have considered everything that needs to be considered.

The exercise is to take the $2600 in your league, and assign it to 230 players who will be taken during your auction. We will give two analogies to illustrate the process of player valuation: business valuation and the "game of chance" valuation.

Business valuation is the closest parallel to player valuation. A player is a package of value, involving future events that are unknown (but can be reasonably estimated) at the time you do your valuation. When you value a company or a property, you go through various steps. One of the most obvious steps is that you look at recent sales of similar assets. The Rotisserie annual tells actual average prices paid in last year's auctions, nationwide, for every player, based on a sample of about 200 leagues. It's no more complicated than looking up a stock price in the newspaper to see the actual price as of yesterday's close. Also, if you want, you can go through actual calculations to see what a player "earned" in the previous season, or half-season, or previous two years on average, or any time period, following the same methods as if you were a doing a valuation for the coming season.

The more important question when you buy a business, or a ballplayer, is what's going to happen in the future. That's why you need a specific statement of what you expect for stats in the coming season. Back in April 1991, it didn't do you much good to know what Carney Lansford "earned" in 1990, what price he sold for in 1990 auctions, or what his long-term track record said about his value. Lansford was seriously disabled before the start of the 1991 season and was essentially worthless.

Continuing the business valuation scenario, you do various calculations after you have formed your vision of the future. A business generates cash flows, and has a residual or liquidation value as well. So you calculate the present discounted value of future cash flows and the current value of proceeds from a contemplated sell-off of assets after you buy the business, and you end up with a precise calculation of value.

You also find that business valuation people know how to deal with uncertainty. When a company is at risk because of increased competition, unstable management, or any other factor, the business valuation process takes these factors into consideration. The net value reflects various adjustment for contingencies. If you looked behind the net dollar value, you would find a "base case" value and also a specific amount deducted to account for risk. There might even be an add-on value, if the risk is near zero, and the company has obvious upside potential.

In Rotisserie player valuation, the best way to handle risk is to deal with it during the auction. Your "base case" is your calculated value, which is almost always different from what you want to bid in an auction, anyway. The next chapter explains how to adjust your bids to reflect risk and other factors.

The business valuation method illustrates two problems that arise whenever you do Rotisserie player valuations:

(1) Your calculated value may be way off, compared to the actual market value of the asset in question. One of the main reasons why there were so many corporate takeovers during the 1980's was that people doing these calculations on businesses, would keep coming up with calculated "answers" showing that many companies were worth much more than the selling price of their stock. So people with money would simply buy the stock, and own the company, at a price far below the calculated value. In one notable case, the mining company AMAX published its own valuation calculations in full page ads

149

in the Wall Street Journal, to assure stockholders that their stock was worth much more than the current selling price; this action helped to prevent a takeover. The point is: you can calculate all you want, but when it's time to buy, calculated value may be far different from the price that buyers pay in the real world.

(2) Even if calculations could somehow reflect market conditions and get at true values, no two people are ever going to come up with exactly the same calculated answer, except by coincidence. There are too many variables involved, and too many choices and assumptions required to reach an answer. Whenever I see calculated values showing "accuracy" to the penny, I become suspicious of the source. Players are never worth $8.72 or $20.39, because you can't bid $8.72 or $20.39. The rules say you have to bid $8 or $9, or choose between $20 and $21. Precision and accuracy are not the same thing. A pitcher who throws ten consecutive pitches exactly belt high, and exactly nine inches outside, has excellent precision, but his accuracy isn't very good.

The other analogy that we want to apply to player valuation, the "game of chance" parallel, emphasizes the importance of context. You may ask the question, "How much is a player worth if he hits .308 with 10 HR, 55 RBI, and 5 SB?" The mechanical, formula-oriented people who "calculate" player values will jump to give you an answer, but they can answer only for the average roster in the average league. It's sort of like answering the question: "How much are three kings worth in a game of stud poker?" You may calculate that, in an average game, three kings will win 85% of the time, and the average pot is $50, so three aces must be worth $50 X .85, or $37.50. All very simple, except that when you play stud poker and see three aces showing in another hand, you can take your calculated value and put it where the sun doesn't shine.

Player valuations, boiled down to simple answers expressed in one number, can be misunderstood and misused. The more you say, "This is the correct value," the more danger there is of misuse. No player has any value, except in the context of an

150

auction with real bidders and real money (or just real "points") being bid. You can't take a player out of context, and assign a value to him, although people keep trying to do that.

VALUATION GUIDELINES

1. You must account for all of the money in the auction. If you have ten teams with $260 each, your total values (excluding any negative players) must add up to $2600. If you end up with $2580 or $2640, don't worry about it; you are within 1% or 2%, which is close enough for bidding purposes. When you get that close, you should stop calculating and start spending time on other matters, like following the news to see which player situations have changed since you started doing your valuation.

2. You must have the correct number of pitchers and hitters with positive value. If your league has ten teams with 14 hitters and 9 pitchers on each team, you want a valuation list that gives you positive value for 140 hitters and 90 pitchers. If you run a little bit over, say 145 hitters or 93 pitchers, don't be too concerned. If your 140th hitter is worth $1, it is very likely that your 141st hitter will also be worth $1, and so will the 142nd. Likewise, the 90th pitcher, the 91st, and the 92nd are all likely to have a $1 value.

3. The last (140th) hitter and the last (90th) pitcher must have a $1 value. No one is going to pay $2 when there is no one bidding against them. And bids of $0 or negative amounts are not allowed. After nine teams have filled out their pitching slots, the last team can buy any pitcher for $1. The last pitcher always sells for $1 in every real auction, unless the bidder has lost track of what's happening or is a fool. You want your player valuations to reflect these realities.

4. The last player in each position "pool" must be worth $1. Many people miss this point, because hitters are somewhat fungible, but it's the same principle as the hitter/pitcher separation. The key point is that there is more than one auction going on. Once you get all your pitchers, you are GONE from the auction for pitchers. The same thing is true of catchers and other positions. There is a bit of overlap, but basically we have a separate auction for catchers, and separate auctions for corner men (1B/3B), middle infielders (2B/SS) and OF's. In every auction, you reach a point where there is only one owner who has a slot open in each pool. That owner is not going to pay $2 or $5 when there is no one bidding against him.

It amazes us that some people can't see how the roster rules affect player values. If you believe that all hitters are interchangeable, then it shouldn't make any difference if the rules require five outfielders, or four, or six. Now try to picture a league that requires only one outfielder per team. With ten teams in the league, the top ten outfielders will all be sought-after. Then the DH/utility slots are likely to be filled with outfielders, because there will be some star players who didn't make the top ten OF list. Then what? Well, you can look for some outfielders who qualify at other positions, but you are still going to end up facing the fact that the vast majority of outfielders simply don't fit onto anybody's roster. If you have a list of 55 outfielders worth $1 or more, you can take the bottom half of that list and throw it away. Also: how much will a superstar outfielder be worth in the one-outfielder league? There won't be that much difference between the best outfielder and the worst outfielder after the rosters are filled ... so you will find that Griffey Junior and Barry Bonds aren't worth $40 apiece; they're only worth about $15 each.

Back in the rules chapter, we mentioned that Rotisserie is designed to create balance from one position to another. This careful design gives an illusion that position rules don't matter when you assign player values. The fact is that the major league talent pool changes from year to year. You may have many good-hitting middle infielders one year and very few the next. If you ignore these differences, in the long run you are going to waste valuable information and lose.

5. You must allocate separate budgets for hitters and pitchers. They do not compete in the same stat categories, so you have to make a policy decision: how much of the total $2600 should you spend pursuing the four hitting categories and how much should you spend on the pitching categories

We say "policy decision," not "calculation," because no one has yet calculated the theoretically correct answer to the question, "How much money should be allocated to hitting and to pitching?" One prominent writer says it's simple: half of all points are awarded for pitching, and half are awarded for hitting, so you should allocate half of the money to each group. Thus, you assign $1300 to pitching and $1300 to hitting, and for 9 pitchers you end up with and average $14 value for pitchers and an average value of $9 for hitters.

This 50/50 approach is appealing in its simplicity, but it ignores the fact that pitching performances are highly unpredictable. When you build a Rotisserie roster, or assemble an investment portfolio, or run a business, you don't want risk. People pay to avoid risk. You buy insurance, for example. Predictability, on the other hand, has value. "Blue chip" stocks often sell for more than the calculated value of the underlying assets and cash flows, because the companies are stable. People are willing to pay extra for stability. In Rotisserie, most owners are willing to pay extra for hitters and pay less for pitchers. Someday, someone (probably an insurance underwriter by profession) will give us the correct calculations to discount pitcher values and enhance hitter values, but no one has done it yet.

Another writer says that 70/30 is the correct hitting/pitching allocation, because three of the eight categories (batting average, ERA, and BPI ratio) should be assigned zero value, while the other five categories deserve all the attention when you allocate money. Thus hitters end up with three "meaningful" categories, while pitchers have only two, and the arithmetics works through to 70/30.

The error of this theory is the assumption that the "average" hitter has a zero value in the BA category, because those in the top half have positive value, and those in the bottom half have negative value, and the category as a whole is worth zero. The average hitter does not have a zero value in batting average. If the

BA for the whole league is .265, and you have a whole team of .265 hitters, you don't get a zero in batting average. You get five or six points. With an average BA, you are in the middle of the pack, not at the bottom. The 70/30 theory cannot explain where those five or six points come from, or the five or six points each for the team with the average ERA and the average BPI ratio. (Credit Mike Dalecki with first explaining this fallacy in the 70/30 theory.)

Personally, we don't spend a great deal of time trying to calculate the pitcher/hitter allocation. We let the market speak for itself, just as we look in the paper or check the financial cable to see the current prices on stocks and commodities. We are more interested in knowing what happens in actual, real live auctions. The results are astoundingly consistent. Every year, nationwide, people spend 65% of the total auction money on hitting and 35% on pitching. There isn't much variation. Old leagues, new leagues, AL, NL, whatever: fully 90% of all leagues fall within a narrow range of 63% to 67% on hitting, so there's your answer.

Just two more points on the 65/35 answer:

(a) **We are talking about league totals, not spending within your unique roster.** There is nothing wrong with spending 50% of YOUR money on pitching, or 80% of your money on hitting. Indeed, you should always be ready to grab any players at bargain prices, whether they are hitters or pitchers. You can always trade one for the other. The point is simply that you should allocate your TOTAL league $2600 (or $3120) using the 65/35 breakdown to get player values. Once you have your valuation lists, you can buy any players you want.

(b) **The risk factor for pitchers is reduced considerably if have the freedom to activate, demote or waive any pitcher at any time.** Bad pitcher stats are most painful when you simply can't do anything to get the bad pitcher off your roster. When you buy a "good" pitcher, part of the price includes risk avoidance: a lifetime 3.00 ERA may not guarantee a great season, but it gives assurance that a horrible season is less likely than would be the case if the pitcher had a 4.50 lifetime ERA.

154

If you play by the rules of Rotisserie Ultra, or have other rules that allow easy removal of bad pitchers, you can allocate less money to pitching. In an Ultra auction, you can allocate 70% or even 75% to hitters, and then wait to see which pitchers emerge to have good seasons, which ones collapse, and change your selections as the season unfolds. We have more on the special considerations for Ultra in Volume II.

THE VALUATION "RECIPE"

The following process is illustrated with actual examples in Volume II. The general flow, without the numbers, is:

1. Separate your pitching/hitting money, as described above.

2. Sort all players by position. If you have your player names and forecast stats on a computer disk, put one assigned position (1B, 2B etc.) next to each player's name.

Whether you are scratching notes on paper or using a computer, you need to know who qualifies at what position, before you can start drafting or bidding. Many players qualify at multiple positions. The standard rule is that, if a player played 20 or more games at that position last year, if he played that position more than any other, or if he has already played that position this year before draft day, then he qualifies. For reasons explained below, you should initially assign positions according to the probable scarcity of talent at each position. Every player qualified at multiple position should be clearly indicated as such, because you might need that information during the draft.

Until you get into your draft or auction, you can't tell exactly which positions are going to be toughest to fill. In 1991, we saw a league almost run out of qualified shortstops, because several people chose a SS for their middle infield (either 2B or SS) position, and some put shortstops at their "any/utility" position. We actually came within one name of running out of qualified shortstops; Dave Anderson was the last one left. After him, we don't know what we would have done. Anyway, the point is to know multiple eligibilities, because you might need them.

The probable scarcity, and the order in which you should assign position eligibilities, is as follows. First, classify every player who qualifies at catcher. Second, identify everyone who qualifies at a middle infield position; it doesn't make much difference, because they are somewhat interchangeable, but we mark shortstops first, and then second basemen. Third, you identify corner infielders (We mark the third basemen, then the first basemen.) Finally come the outfielders who don't qualify at any other position.

3. Total the number of "units" in each stat category. If you are valuing 1993, add up the total number of home runs, RBI, etc. in your forecast stats for 1993 for all players. For batting average, the unit is a base hit that elevates you in the standings. If the worst team batting average in you league is .250, then every hit by which a player exceeds .250 will be one unit. In the pitching categories, the units for ERA and BPI ratio are innings, to the extent that IP exceed the number of earned runs and baserunners that would be given up by the average pitcher on the last place team in your league. Some players will have negative value in batting average, ERA, and BPI ratio. A few players will have a negative value even after you add in the value of other categories, if they have a very bad BA, ERA, or ratio.

4. Spread the allocated money for pitchers and hitters among the available stat units. Then add up a value for each player.

5. Make adjustments to account for the number of players required at each position. Our method begins with an arbitrary total of much more than $2600 or $3120, so that every player's value is initially inflated. You can then remove value from all players, a little more or less depending on their positions, until you get down to the correct total of $2600 (ten teams) or $3120 (twelve teams). Again, the details are explained in Volume II.

6. Make a few final "sanity" checks. Go back to the four points under "Valuation Guidelines" above.

Aside from these basics, your main effort is to know your own personal league economics. Every league is different. If you have two owners both convinced that Choo Choo Coleman is worth $30, and both of these owners have $30 to spend when Choo Choo's name comes up, he is going to sell for $30. And if NOBODY believed that Choo Choo was worth more than $1, nobody is going to bid $2 or $3 when his name comes up.

We will refer to value calculations repeatedly when you get into the subject of draft tactics and strategies in the next chapter.

Prepare as well as you can and then get a good night's sleep, so you'll be ready to go on draft day.

9TH INNING

DRAFT DAY: FINAL PREPARATIONS

> *"Baseball is the most intellectual game because most of the action goes on in your head."*
> *- Henry Kissinger*

THE LINEUP

- When is it time to stop preparing for the big day?
- Which tools should you have available?
- Should you bring a partner or two with you?
- What important tasks should you concentrate on during the draft?

Some people never want to stop preparing. We know one owner who takes a transistor radio into the draft room, just to make sure he doesn't miss any late-breaking news. There is surely some value in knowing if a star player breaks his leg during your draft, but the chance of that happening is fairly remote. On balance, the distraction of ongoing news is probably not a good idea. Our friend with the radio has never drafted a seriously-injured player in six years, but he hasn't won his league in six years, either. Our advice is to find a colleague who will follow the news for you and provide any necessary updates, while you concentrate on assembling a great roster.

At some point, you must shift your attention away from

preparation and start deciding which players you want, and how much you want them. It is vital to have your mind focused entirely on the player selection process. Preparation is necessary for success in a draft, but once you get to the first name in the first round, you are engaged in an all-absorbing struggle where the key factors are concentration, memory, personal organization, quick-thinking, perception, ability to see every decision from your opponents' point of view, and (last but not least) stamina.

If you haven't been in a draft before, you are in for a real treat.* Every draft has its own life. There will be twists and turns and surprises every minute. Your draft will develop its own sense of humor and its own competitive sub-plots, as people seize on themes and enhance them hour after hour. From an amusement point of view, there is nothing quite like a Rotisserie draft. If you let your imagination conjure up an image of the most fun you have ever had playing any sport or game, combined with an exciting social occasion, you will begin to get a feeling for what is involved in a Rotisserie draft.

As an intellectual competition, there are numerous parallels that come close to describing what's involved in a draft. The concentration level is right up there with tournament chess and bridge. The competitive excitement is similar to high stakes poker. The intellectual strain is comparable to a tough, six-hour final exam, something like taking the college entrance exams or the law boards. From our own experience, we can tell you: it is easier to manage your way through the CPA exam than to maintain your focus through a Rotisserie draft (and the CPA exam is designed to hit you with all kinds of new and different questions, just to see if you can keep your head while not being dogmatic). The single phrase that seems to carry over from the academic world and apply to Rotisserie draft performance is "exam generalship."

*We have referred to a draft throughout the first part of this chapter, although most of the same tactics apply to an auction. The middle part of the chapter refers primarily to the auction process; then the draft is discussed again at the end.

There is no scoreboard during a draft, so the participants can only guess how well they are doing at any point in time. At the end of the draft, most people have a distorted view of how well they did. There is a phenomenon that we call the "inverse ignorance ratio" in self assessment. Smarter owners generally focus on all their missed opportunities and mistakes, and they see the good moves made by others; people with good rosters usually feel bad at the end of their draft. The less astute owners are more likely to be pleased with their rosters; they got the one or two players who were at the top of their "want list" (no matter what the price) and won't see the error of their ways until the season is half finished.

So when the time comes, you must become fully absorbed in the draft. Still, there are some final items of preparation that must be completed, after you finish your scouting, forecasting and valuation, but before you start putting names on your roster. You can help yourself by taking some last steps to get ready for the draft itself:

1. PLAN YOUR DECISION-MAKING PROCESS

"Process?" you may ask. "What process?" If you simply take a list of players and values to your draft, and keep choosing names until your roster is full, that doesn't take a lot of planning, does it? No, but you are not going to win that way, either. Winning takes a little foresight and effort.

First, consider whether you can bring a friend or partner with you. Some leagues don't allow partners to help during the big day, but most of them tolerate or even encourage the presence of colleagues and assistants. If you can bring along another person or two, that could be a big advantage. The best-functioning team I ever saw had three people doing separate jobs. One of them kept track of which players were taken and which were available. Another kept track of how much money each team had spent and what positions remained vacant at all times. The third person sat at the draft table and actually did the bidding for players; he was especially responsible for studying the faces of the other owners and looking for bluffs, anxiety, and opportunities.

Randy B.: Our league has a scoreboard in the front of the room. It shows how much money is available for each team, players bought, salaries and positions. This has proven very helpful to the less experienced owners, although I prefer draft software to do the job for me. You can do fine in an auction without a computer, but it certainly can be used to your advantage.

Three participants per team could put 36 people in a draft room and we admit that sounds a little excessive. But you shouldn't overlook the fact that an ally or two can help. If you bring someone with you, it is vital to have a clear division of labor and to work out your roles before going to the draft. In case you are thinking of it, don't try changing roles in the middle of a draft, even if you are 50/50 partners. You will both destroy your concentration and end up doing worse.

After partnership, another big question is whether your league allows computers in the draft room. Many leagues prohibit computers. Most of those prohibitions sprung up in the mid-1980's when a good laptop PC cost about $6000. Since more people now have portable computers, more leagues are beginning to tolerate them. The key point is that you should know what your league allows, make your preparation match the league's general practice and try to influence the rule yourself if you have a preference.

If you are a beginner at Rotisserie baseball or if you don't use computers in your daily life, you should favor a rule that keeps them out of the draft room. To get competitive benefit from computers during a draft, you need some practical experience in previous drafts and auctions, and you also need to know how to put your computer to work for you. Even when you become good at Rotisserie and proficient with computers, you need good software to get a competitive edge. The best software (in our humble opinion) is the package that bears John's name. It is available by calling 203-834-0812.

2. HAVE YOUR TOOLS READY

The following information is essential for preparation:

(a) You need one master list of players available on which you will indicate or cross off players as they are taken. This list should indicate position eligibility and your dollar values, if you are having an auction. You must be able to see instantly who is available and this list must be flawless throughout the auction. If you don't list every available player before you start, you are just wasting information that is available with little cost or effort. Note that you should have only one primary list showing players taken. If you have various lists, sorted by position, sorted in alphabetical order, etc., and try to cross off players taken on all these lists, you will waste valuable effort. You will take attention away from the draft by trying to keep multiple lists current.

(b) You need a list of players sorted by eligible position. The master list mentioned above could be sorted by position or you could have subsidiary lists. Within each position listing, you should rank the players from top to bottom and show the dollar value for each name. (Assign dollar values even if you are not following the auction format; you will see why shortly.)

(c) You need a roster worksheet for each of your opponents, on which you can enter the players taken and see at a glance which positions are filled and which are vacant. One bid sheet with a column for each roster will do the job nicely. You can quickly glance down a roster and see which positions are vacant and you can quickly look across each position row to see which teams have vacancies.

(d) You need a worksheet showing money spent and money remaining for each team, if you use an auction. The "money" sheet can be the same as the roster list described in (c) above. Obviously, you need a sharp pencil or a fine point pen, because you will have to write small.

(e) In addition to these "must" lists, you will probably want various other lists that will be useful in certain situations during the draft. Some of these will be obvious when you read our advice on draft tactics. Examples of the popular lists are:

• "Likely Overbid" players, e.g. last year's World Series heroes, last year's top starting pitchers, highly-publicized rookies, all rookie pitchers who are supposed to be good and older players who were top stars five years ago.

• "Safe Pitchers" (low value, low risk, basically a bunch of low-ERA middle relievers).

• Injured players (any list from a newspaper or injury update service will do) so you can see at a glance who has what wrong with them.

• If you have an auction, players you plan to nominate early. These should generally be names you have little or no interest in. This will help you find bargains later in the auction.

• Fake lists: with all these lists floating around, somebody is going to look over your shoulder sometime during the draft; it happens in every league, unavoidably. Make a list that includes a mixture of players you like and players you don't like; put circles and arrows around a couple who you don't like.

If your draft is in a relatively small, crowded room, arrange your lists to reflect that fact. Recognize that you can't spread out too much. Get a clipboard so you won't be dropping your lists or getting them mixed up. Put your fake list on top. Practice flipping through your lists before the draft, so you won't have to go through a learning curve after the action starts. If your draft is run by phone or remote computer and you have complete privacy, take advantage of that fact. Cover your walls like a "war room" full of useful information.

The image of all these lists to keep track of during the draft might make your head spin, especially if you haven't done it before. To be sure, it is possible to overdo your list making and to end up with a lot of paper that isn't useful.

164

Here are a few ideas to keep things under control:

• For your first draft or auction, use just one master list, sorted by position and by value within position. In future years, you can add other lists after you have perceived a need for them.

• If something has to give, let it be keeping track of other people's money. You will give up a small competitive edge by not knowing every owner's financial condition at every moment, but it's better to give up a little edge than to become totally confused. Anytime when you find yourself losing track of who's been taken, you are trying to do too much. **Concerning money, beginners should lobby to have their league's auctioneer keep a running tab and review it frequently during the auction.**

• Use combinations and overlays to consolidate your lists. Colored highlight pens are extremely useful. Using just the one master list, for example, you could highlight players you want to bring up for bid early in orange, highlight pitchers who are OK but not great with yellow, highlight sleepers with blue, etc.

3. ARRIVE AT YOUR DRAFT RESTED AND FOCUSED

Take a break and clear your head sometime before the draft. Get a good night's sleep. One of the world's greatest Rotisserians, John Tippler, will never win his league, because he doesn't follow this advice. John's fellow owners know that he likes to party. So, for the past eight years, they have always found a way to see that he is suitably amused the night before draft day. Poor John goes to spring training, studies intensely, prepares copious lists loaded with insight and always finishes fourth or fifth because of a bad draft.

Some people need to put away their player lists and rankings for a full day or two. The more homework you have done, the longer you need to relax and get your mind clear. Even those of you who have just pulled together a few notes on the morning before the draft are well advised to take a half hour respite before it actually starts. If you see someone pouring over his lists as he walks into the draft room, you are probably looking at a loser.

We don't advocate taking a vacation to the extent that you might miss vital news, but you could consider taking your spouse out for dinner on the night before draft day (she won't see you again for six months, you know); just get back in time to catch the baseball news on TV. On draft day, you can benefit from taking a ten minute walk and breathing some fresh air before getting started. The point is: don't be talking to yourself or re-ranking players when you sit down to start drafting. Be ready and be sharp.

CONDUCT OF THE AUCTION

One of main benefits of good preparation is that it makes you relaxed and confident. If you haven't been to an auction before, you should get one point perfectly clear: **EVERYBODY in the auction is going to make mistakes. Good preparation will help you minimize your mistakes, but you can never eliminate them entirely.** During the auction, it is critical to put mistakes behind you, moment by moment, and focus on the next problem. Never let yourself waste even one second brooding. You have the whole summer to feel sorry for yourself; use your time for choosing players thoughtfully.

ROTISSERIE RECOMMENDATION
Do not go to an auction believing that you must buy
any particular player.

It is OK to have a list of, say, five or ten power hitters of which you "must" get at least one, and five or ten ace relievers from which you plan to get one, etc. But it is not OK to go to your auction thinking, "I must get Cecil Fielder." You can do that if you want to of course, but you will be playing for the fun of owning Cecil Fielder, not for the fun of winning your league. Take your pick.

While you are trying to keep your own mistakes to a

minimum, you can do all kinds of things to help your opponents make large and frequent errors. It takes a little experience to learn which people are most susceptible to which kinds of errors, but there are some general themes that are almost always successful strategies:

1. Sit back during the early stages of your auction.

One of the great truisms of Rotisserie auctions is that prices are higher in the beginning. Then everyone has plenty of money to spend and everyone has a vacancy at every position — so everyone can bid on every player. During the early stages of the auction, you don't want to buy players. You hope that the players you want will not come up early; you hope they will come up near the end of the auction.

When it's your turn to nominate a player early in the auction, bring up someone likely to be in demand, generating bids in excess of value. You want to focus on players who are most difficult to value, e.g. rookies, starting pitchers in general, players who have just had surprising seasons (either good or bad), players who have changed teams (or better yet, changed leagues) and anyone who is doing anything new or different, such as playing a new position or playing for a new manager.

Some types of players are almost always overvalued. Here are some ideas to help you stimulate excessive bids by your opponents:

• Last year's World Series heroes are always popular; everybody loves a winner. The more publicity they received, the more overbidding their names will generate.

• Hometown favorites are sure bets to attract high bids. Focus especially on the most promising youngsters and the starting pitchers on your hometown team.

• Bring up your opponents' favorite players, regardless of team. The single most important competitive intelligence that you can collect before your draft is: who are the favorite players of each of the other owners?

• Think of rookies who have received the most publicity. Visualize magazine covers, Rookie All Star Teams in the major newspapers, the most recent Minor League Player of the Year, hot baseball cards, etc.

• Nominate pitchers who were top starters (especially Cy Young winners) about three or four years ago. You want famous names.

The ploy of bringing up names you don't want will usually work consistently through the first third of an auction (about eight rounds), sometimes longer. In Volume II, we show you how to know exactly when people have stopped overpaying. Even as a beginner, you will get a feel for that point, when you see two or three consecutive players sell for a "fair" price or go as bargains.

There is one important rule to keep in mind when bringing up players you don't want: never bid $1 on anyone unless you are willing to take them for $1. There is no assurance that someone is going to take you off the hook. You might think that someone should always be willing to pay $2 for the pitcher who won the Cy Young award four years ago, but if he had ERA's over six in both of the past two seasons, you might be the only person bidding.

2. Look for bargains.

The players likely to sell for less than they are worth are the opposites of those types listed above. What's the opposite of a home town favorite? A hated rival, of course. If you live in Boston, Yankees will usually be cheap. If you live in San Francisco, the bargains will be Dodgers and in LA the Giants will possibly be underappreciated.

Who's the opposite of famous? The tiny media markets are great places to look for auction day bargains. Players from San Diego, Seattle, Milwaukee, Houston and the other smaller cities will be the best bargains.

Who's the opposite of a rookie pitcher? A veteran hitter, of course. Some of the best bargains are those unexciting, never All-Star, regular players who just keep getting 500 at bats, year after year. You don't want a fancy-fielding shortstop with a .220 lifetime batting average, but a second baseman who consistently hits .245 with 8 homers, 40 RBI, and 11 SB will usually be underappreciated, unless he has done something to attract attention.

Who's the opposite of a World Series hero? A nobody on a losing team fits the bill pretty well. You want the opposite of fame. To find these players, look for at bat totals that surprise you on the high side. When you find yourself thinking, "What? He got 480 at bats last year and the year before? I thought he was a bench jockey," then you have found yourself a candidate for a bargain.

3. Wait for the "end game."

Just as players sell for too much during the early rounds, they sell for too little near the end. This whole phenomenon exists in all leagues, but is very much at work in leagues with several beginners doing the bidding. We can remember one auction back in 1988, when the astute Brian Spectacle kept very careful track of money and rosters, and said, "Vince Coleman, $2," in the twentieth round. All the people who had enough money to bid $3 didn't have any outfield or utility slots open, and everyone who had a vacant slot couldn't bid $3.

Remember to try to save some money for the end, so that you don't finish up taking bums for $1 apiece when you could be buying genuine stars for $3 or $4. You don't want to be left with lots of money and no talent to spend it on, but you don't want to miss the bargains at the end, either. If you do a good job of not spending too much early and a decent job of keeping track, you should be in good shape at the end of the auction.

4. Knock out other teams toppers' rights.

If your league has toppers' rights, you don't want those toppers (except your own of course) coming into play near the end of the auction when prices are low. You want people to pay the highest possible prices if and when they exercise their toppers' rights. Obviously, you want to bring up other people's best topper players as early as possible, when prices will be high.

John B: In the CompuServe Palmer league of 1991, I went

into the auction with a large collection of topper rights that I had carefully assembled through winter trading. Much to my dismay, I found that all my toppers' were blown off within the first few rounds. I felt like the Iraqi air defense system during the first few minutes of Desert Storm: boom, boom, gone.

Randy B.: In our league, we auction all the Toppers' players first (by last year's salaries from highest to lowest). This is a good rule for less experienced leagues, since the owners have one less problem to resolve.

OPTIMAL BIDDING

Another axiom of auction economics is that people are going to have different opinions of what each player is worth. A few years ago John published a study of actual prices paid in a hundred auctions nationwide and highlighted the case of Alvin Davis for example. Davis, at the time, was a model of consistent performance. He was worth exactly $20 according to every method of calculating value, and sure enough, $20 was the average price paid for Alvin Davis. But if you looked at all these auctions, you could see that Alvin cost as much as $37 in one auction and sold for $25 to $30 in many. On the low end, he was available for $16 or less in about one fifth of all auctions and he sold for $10 or less in about one eighth of them.

Whenever a player sells for more than you think he's worth, that's good news for you. In a new league with twelve teams and $260 per team, you start the auction with a rational list that shows 276 players worth $1 or more and $3120 in total value for all these players. When a $10 player (on your list) sells for $20 (which may have been the value on someone else's list), you now see $3000 of money remaining and players worth $3010. Then if a $5 player sells for $10, your list shows talent worth $3005 still remaining, but only $2990 left to spend. Simply stated, prices are bound to fall; there is less money chasing more talent every time someone overpays. Near the end of the auction, you may find

$200 worth of talent remaining and only $15 of cash still in circulation; the bargains are imminent.

This phenomenon works from your point of view, even if everyone else is rational. Other people assign value to players who you think are worthless. After the auction ends, some of the players that you thought were worth $1, $2 or even $5 will remain untaken, because people came to the auction with different ideas of who was valuable and who wasn't. Among the players who were taken, there were differing opinions about how much each was worth.

From your point of view, much money is wasted in every auction. Just by glancing at any record of actual prices paid in last year's auctions, such as in the annual review published by Heath Research (804-498-8197), you will find numerous prices that approach absurdity. The reason is that you have not only differences of opinion about value, but you also have people bidding irrationally, e.g. "I don't care if I win, I just want to own Cecil Fielder."

On average, the median price paid in a large number of auctions is exactly equal to true value. But that means half the time people are paying too much and half the time they are paying too little. The quantity of wasted money is very large and can be measured accurately.

Easier than counting "wasted" dollars and re-calculating values, you can tell the probability (using nationwide averages) that you will succeed in buying a player at 90% of value, 80% of value, 50% of value, etc. For example, a star hitter can be bought for under 80% of value about one fifth of the time. That may not sound like much frequency, but it means (roughly) that if you bid 75% of value on five star hitters, you will probably get one of them.

Four times out of five, the optimal bid (say, 80% of the calculated value of a start hitter) won't work. However, patience and flexibility will yield profits. You have to be patient, but you can't be picky about buying your favorite players.

You know your "profit" when you buy a player. If you

obtain a $20 (calculated) value for $14, that's a $6 profit. Optimal bids can be calculated by simply taking each incremental price ($1, $2, $3, etc.) and for each price, listing the possible profit ($) and the probability of getting that player at that price. We can tell you the probability, based on hundreds of auctions nationwide. A $6 profit, with 20% probability of a successful bid, means that you have an Expected Value of $1.20: (0.20 probability X $6.00 potential profit). Every time you bid $14 on a $20 star hitter, you have an average profit of $1.20. Four times out of five, you buy nothing, but one time out of five, you have a $6 profit.

If you bid higher, you increase the probability of buying a player, but you decrease the profit. If you bid lower, you decrease the probability but increase the possible profit. The optimal bid is simply the point at which your multiplication (probability times profit) yields the highest answer.

The conclusion of optimal bidding studies is that you should try very, very hard to bid no more than 85% of a player's calculated value. Unless the player is a star hitter or an established ace reliever, you shouldn't be bidding more than 70% of calculated value. By refusing to bid higher, you will accumulate money for the end of the auction, when prices drop.

John B.: I receive dozens of letters from people every summer, telling me the same story: "After many years of finishing near the bottom, I finally tried optimal bidding. I sat through the auction and didn't buy ANY players until the fifteenth round. It was painful. People kept looking at me and teasing me. All my favorite players were already sold by the time I started bidding. I got a bunch of no-names. I am in first place by a wide margin. Now everybody thinks I'm a genius. Thank you."

BUDGETING

Optimal bidding is the most useful tool that you can bring to an auction, but you need more. If your league is well-established with a high level of competition, the bids are going

172

to be in a narrower range than what you find in the "average" league. It is conceivable that you could come to the end of your auction and find that the remaining excess value is for low-value players. In other words, you might be able to get several players worth $5 or more for $1 apiece at the end of the auction. However, you might be unable to spend all your money because there aren't enough high value players left to bid on.

The last thing you want to do is finish the auction with much unspent money. You want to pack as much value as possible onto your roster. To do that, you might have to pay up to full, calculated value for certain players in certain situations. These situations are most likely to arise in ongoing leagues where most of the good players have been retained and won't be available in the auction. We have generally put material for experienced leagues in Volume II. That is where you will find examples of roster budgeting (allocating certain dollar amounts to certain positions).

A beginner or a new league is not likely to need much work on budgeting, but we are introducing the subject here so you can start thinking about it. The basic idea is that you need certain components somewhere on your roster in order to win. For a new league you should look at all the available players and count how many are worth $20 or more. If you see 36 defined "stars" in your twelve-team league, your fair share would be three of the star players.

For simplicity, assume we are talking about players worth $20 to $40 apiece, $30 on average, in the star category. (You can find the actual numbers by looking at your own value lists for your own league.) In this example, if you have $260 to spend on your whole team, then these three players might cost you an average of $30 apiece or $90 in total.

At the start of your auction, you need to allocate $90 for these three star players. That doesn't mean you intend to pay $90 for them; you hope to obtain $90 worth of talent in these three players, while paying under $75. But you should recognize at the outset that you MIGHT need $90.

173

Obviously, you need a list of players who meet the "star" criteria. You may have a definition other than "worth $20 or more." In fact, you can make this as complicated as you want. You can have separate budgets for "superstar hitters," "high value outfielders" or any other categories that you choose to define, and your budgets and categories can overlap.

In this simple example, just picture a budget of up to $90 for three "high value" players. Remember, you cannot set your sights on any particular player, so you should make a list of about thirty-five players who qualify for this category. The longer your list of acceptable candidates, the better you are going to do. And you have to be flexible. Your top candidate might have a calculated value of $40. With a long list, you might include players worth $19 or $18.

You have to use judgment and keep track of who's available. Until you reach the end of your list, you should just wait. But when you see that you are down to the last few players from your pre-defined star list, you should start bidding aggressively, up to 100% of calculated value.

If you miss all of the "good" players in the star category, you must make two changes: (1) you should start bidding aggressively on players who come close to meeting the standards you have set for each category and (2) you should shift some of your $90 "star" budget to the remaining players. For example, if you were pressed into spending $30 each for two stars and you don't have anyone else worth over $10, you can allocate the unspent $30 to buy two $15 players, even though you had previsouly planned to buy one $29 player and one $1 player.

While making these changes in tactics, you still shouldn't bid over full, calculated value for any player. NEVER! You don't need any $30 players to win your league. If you end up with a bunch of $15 players who you bought for prices like $4 or $6, you should be able to easily trade your bargain-priced regular players for high-priced superstars later in the year.

The main point of roster budgeting is that you want to start the season with a foundation of highly-valued talent. Note that we say "want to" and not "have to." During the auction, you need to recognize situations when it is appropriate to bid up to full value. Budgeting is the easiest method to help you recognize those situations.

DRAFT INFLATION

The above discussion of "value" is based on a new league with all teams having empty rosters. An ongoing league with retained players will almost always have some amount of "draft inflation."

Simply stated, **draft inflation occurs when the value of players retained exceeds the salaries at which these players are retained.** Each owner keeps his best bargain-priced players, so he will have more money for the auction. If you retain a player worth $20 for a salary of $10, you are removing more talent than money. It's exactly the opposite of what happens early in an auction when people are overpaying for players. By retaining players at favorable salaries, everyone is, in effect, starting the auction with a number of bargain purchases. **When the auction starts, there is less talent and more money, so prices must be adjusted upward.** Volume II tells you how to make that adjustment.

THE SIMPLE DRAFT-PICK METHOD

If your league selects players with a simple rotating draft, your draft day is going to be much simpler than if you have an auction. You can live without optimal bids or roster budgeting and you don't have to keep track of your money or anyone else's. You only have to name players and they are yours. However, the "simple" draft has its own complexities and unique twists and turns.

As we said in the rules discussion, the draft usually does a better job of separating and rewarding those who are well prepared. So the first priority is to make thorough lists and rankings at each position. In an auction format you can nominate any name at a price of $1 and hope that somebody will take you off the hook if the player is a bum. At least it's possible that you can be saved. In a draft, once you name a player, he's on your roster.

Your objective during a draft isn't very complicated. You simply have to identify the best player available each time it's your turn. The only reason you have to watch your opponents is because their actions might affect your definition of "best" at any moment.

Here are important draft principles:

1. Focus on Position Scarcity.

The key objective in a draft format is to make sure that you don't get shut out and miss all the good players at any position. The scarcest player type is the ace reliever; they often disappear within the first few rounds. The "skill positions" of catcher, shortstop, and (to a lesser extent in most years) third base and second base, all receive special attention, also.

When making a selection, the question that you want to ask yourself is: "If I don't get this particular player now, who is going to be available at my next turn?" This is when dollar values can help you, even though you aren't having an auction. Each player's dollar value also answers the question: "What happens if I don't obtain any of the "good" players and end up with the last guy at this position?" A $25 player, by definition, is worth $24 more than the last man at that position.

Suppose you look at your list of outfielders and see the next eight available players are worth $25, $25, $24, $24, $23, $22, $21 and $21, respectively. You shouldn't feel any sense of urgency about grabbing the top outfielder. Now suppose you look at shortstops and your available list shows the top shortstop is worth $19, the second best is $11 and the rest are worth $9 or less. In this situation, you should probably choose the $19 shortstop, not the $25 outfielder. In the shortstop pool, you can see a drop of $8 or more following the next shortstop selection.

In the outfield pool, you are not likely to lose more than $4 in value by waiting until the next round.

Keeping track of other teams' rosters is especially critical in a draft. In the above example, you might want to look deeper than eight players on your available outfielders list. If there will be twenty picks before you choose again and most of the other teams have three or four vacancies for outfielders while their shortstop positions are almost all filled, the $25 outfielder might be the better selection (usually not, but he might be). You need judgment and good luck, but the point to keep in mind is simple: try to foresee what will happen if you don't take the highest-valued player on your list. Very often, taking a player with a lower "raw" value is a better idea.

Knowing that a team has filled a particular position can give you a big advantage. Suppose, for example, that you are trying to choose between two players in the fifteenth round. Both have a value of $9 according to your list. One is a shortstop and the other is a third baseman. Say you are picking in the ninth position in a twelve-team draft. The tenth, eleventh and twelfth teams will choose after you. Then the order reverses and the twelfth, eleventh and tenth teams will choose again, and then it's back to your turn. If you examine the rosters and see that these other three teams are all filled at shortstop, middle infield and utility, your answer is simple: you take the third baseman, knowing that the shortstop will be available next time.

Ace relievers are even more important than shortstops and catchers. In an auction, you can react to the ace reliever situation as it unfolds by bidding aggressively if and when it becomes necessary. But in a draft, you can find yourself cut off from the saves category and be helpless to do anything about it. Every draft has a life of its own and you have to watch what other people are doing. However, as a general rule, you should aim to obtain one ace reliever among your first five picks and try for another before the tenth round. If you have both AL and NL teams to choose from, you can wait just a little longer before you are shut out, but you also need twice as many ace relievers to get your fair

177

share. Just figure there is one ace reliever per major league team and count how many there will be in your draft.

2. Put the squeeze on other teams.

While you are trying to get the most out of your own draft picks, look for opportunities to diminish the value of other teams' draft picks. Focus especially on teams that you perceive as rivals, if you think you are a contender.

One general tactic is that you want to be a leader not a follower, when choosing which position to fill. When there have just been several picks of starting pitchers, don't take a starting pitcher (unless you see one who is head and shoulders above all of those who were just selected). You will be conceding a deficit compared to the other teams when you take the next-best player. After several owners take pitchers, go for the best available hitter. After a run on outfielders, take the best infielder or the best relief pitcher. Throughout the auction, keep asking yourself: "Which position hasn't been mentioned for a long time?" And check your list for that position before making your selection. You will find various pleasant surprises.

If you don't allow other teams to put the squeeze on you, it means you are successfully putting the squeeze on the other owners. You can be aggressive along these lines. If you see that seven teams haven't yet taken a shortstop and the best available shortstops are worth $7, $6, $4, $3, $1 and $1, respectively, you could start a run on shortstops by taking the one worth $7. If the other teams are paying attention, the next three picks might be those three shortstops worth $6, $4 and $3. You will have locked in a profit relative to those who picked after you and you will have condemned some teams to living with $1 shortstops (which can be painful).

3. Don't jump at starting pitchers early.

If you choose one ace starter within your first eight or ten picks, that's enough. There are many more starting pitchers than any other position, so you won't see big drops in value when you ask that question: "What happens if I don't take the best available SP now?" In a roundabout way, waiting for starting pitchers in a draft is like allocating your money in favor of hitters in an auction.

At the end of the draft, don't grab a group of bad starters, even if you have a strict innings pitched requirement. It is safer to pick harmless middle relievers and then trade for starting pitchers after you see which ones are likely to have good seasons. If you don't invest heavily in starting pitchers, you will be strong in hitting and relief pitching, so owners should come to you with trade proposals.

In summary, whether you use a draft or an auction, the main idea is to pack as much value as possible onto your roster. You don't need "balance," although it's nice. The end of the draft means you are beginning a six-month journey on roster management and you want to be well-supplied at the start.

Having the best books, magazines, computer programs and other tools is an important key to winning.

10TH INNING
TOOLS FOR WINNING

To win any sport or game, you need the right equipment. In this chapter, we tell you our ideas about the best equipment for winning at Rotisserie baseball. A few of the notices are blatantly commercial, but we wouldn't be advising you to buy them if we didn't believe in them fervently. Remember that you need to take advantage of any accurate information you can find to win your league; make sure other owners don't prepare better than you do for the upcoming season. It's beyond your control if you lose because of bad luck — however, it's a different story if another team claims victory because of better information.

NEWSPAPERS

For a daily newspaper, we recommend USA TODAY in addition to your local daily. USA is the only paper that covers every major league city. Out-of-town newspapers are also excellent sources of valuable articles.

For weekly reading, there are two excellent choices, USA TODAY Baseball Weekly and The Sporting News. John writes a Rotisserie column for Baseball Weekly.

Baseball America, a bi-weekly publication, provides great converage of the minor leagues. It also provides day-to-day developments in the majors, as well as winter league and spring training information.

For monthly reading, you want Winning Rotisserie Baseball, the journal for serious competitors. (See page 182.)

WINNING ROTISSERIE BASEBALL
(Monthly!)
by John Benson

When a player gets hurt, traded, demoted or called up during the season, you know all about it from the newspapers and TV. But does the media tell you the other players who will be affected? And how? Who will play while Davis is on the DL and how long will Davis be out? Why did Chicago trade for Jones and how will they use their new acquisition? Who will replace Martinez and what is the new batting order? Why was the rookie Smith brought up? Will he play? Who will sit down to make room for him?

These are the types of questions that are answered every month in WINNING ROTISSERIE BASEBALL, the first, best and largest publication for serious readers on this subject. John's mission is to give you an informed vision of the future. Fifty writers cover the major and minor leagues for you. Highlights include:

• Comprehensive post spring-training Draft Day issue.

• More detailed lists like the "Age 26 with 2+ years ML experience" population.

• Final wrap-up of winter ball every year.

• Complete list of all players who changed teams during the winter, and the likely effect of the change on the player, his old team and his new team.

• Continuous updates all through the season: who's hot, who's not, who to grab, who to dump.

A sample issue is $7. A six month subscription is $35. One year is $59. Two years is $99. WINNING ROTISSERIE BASEBALL comes with a complete 100% money back guarantee. Telephone 203-834-0812 or write to Diamond Analytics, PO Box 7302, Wilton, CT 06897.

FANTASY BASEBALL MAGAZINE

If you like Rotisserie information, you can now receive it four times a year in a colorful, clear and attractive presentation. Greg Ambrosius oversees the delivery of timely and useful essays, stats, rankings and analyses. Don't tell them we said this, but their magazine is terribly inexpensive. It's as good as any value in the industry.

It has been fun and personally rewarding to see FBB Magazine evolve since late 1989. Every issue has been better than the ones that went before, and the energy and enthusiasm that go into each issue make it likely that this trend will continue for a long time. For a subscription call 715-445-2214 or write to 700 E. State St., Iola, WI 54990.

SOFTWARE

John Benson's Draft Software is simply the best, fastest program with the most accurate forecasts and dollar values. It includes the Player Valuation program and Draft Management program. This software is miles ahead of any similar products.

Why suffer on draft day? Let John Benson's Draft Software do all the work for you. Keep track of money and players taken. View any roster. Check the list of available players and see what they are worth to you, at that moment, on your specific roster! This program uses John Benson's forecast stats for the coming season, lets you use last year's stats or you can plug in your own forecast. It includes an automated valuation module and comes with a 50-page user manual.

Just $49.95 plus $2 shipping. Call Diamond Analytics at 1-800-292-6338.

STAT SERVICES

There are many competent, experienced, reasonably-priced stats services scattered throughout the U.S. If you are seeking one of them for your league, there are hundreds of ads in the major Rotisserie publications. An intelligent way to choose a worthy stat service is to poll other owners and leagues for their recommendations. Following are three of our favorites who have proven themselves over the years. They will be thrilled if you contact them for further information.

HEATH RESEARCH. Jerry Heath is a benefactor of writers and researchers. His company publishes the annual Rotisserie Review loaded with draft information, actual prices paid, and standings summaries. Heath Research, 3841 Croonenburgh Way (J), Virginia Beach, Virginia 23452. 804-498-8197.

ROTI-STATS. John Wallwork is a long-time supporter of Rotisserie research and science. John Benson's oldest league uses Roti-Stats and so does Randall Baron's favorite league. Write or call: 11770 Warner Ave., Suite 225, Fountain Valley, CA 92708. 714-668-0158.

ROTISSERIE LEAGUE STATS from the only stats service that is officially authorized by the guys who invented Rotisserie League Baseball®. Contact RLBA 41 Union Square West, Suite 936, New York, NY 10003. 212-695-3463.

FRIENDS OF
ROTISSERIE BASEBALL

ROTISSERIE LEAGUE BASEBALL ASSOCIATION; The game's only official national organization. For a paltry $50 your league receives Official Position Eligibility Lists, 24-Man Major League rosters mailed opening day, commissioner services, Official Championship Certificate, four newsletters, Yoo-Hoo, and one free Official Rotisserie League T-Shirt for your league secretary/commissioner. 41 Union Square West, Suite 936, New York, NY 10003. 212-695-3463.

SOCIETY FOR AMERICAN BASEBALL RESEARCH (SABR): Write Box 470, Garrett Park, MD 20896 or call 301-949-SABR (7227) for information.

STATS ON LINE SERVICE: If you have a computer modem, the STATS database is the ultimate up-to-the-minute news line and historical archive, all in one. Call 708-676-3322 for information.

PHONE SERVICES

GOT A QUESTION? ASK JOHN BENSON! LIVE!
Call "John Benson's Private Line" Just $1.99/minute

Can't decide who to retain? Torn between two free agents? Trade offer keeping you awake at night? Trouble getting your draft list prioritized?

Don't despair. Call for a private, one-on-one chat with the co-author of this book. It's LIVE question and answer, not a tape. You receive patient listening and prompt, clear advice.

The hours are 1 PM to 11 PM daily. During pre-draft season (roughly March 15 to April 15) the line will be open til midnight or even later. This is a busy time of year, so please be patient and persistent. There is only one John Benson.

900-773-7526

JOHN BENSON'S STAT PHONE SERVICE

DAILY BOX SCORES— DAILY INJURY REPORTS
Plus ... JOHN BENSON'S COMMENTARY (ON TAPE)

Who's hot and who's not. Who to grab and who to dump. Updated every Saturday afternoon during the baseball season. Just 99 cents/minute! **900-737-1234**

SPORTS FORUM ON COMPUSERVE

Finding Sports Forum on CompuServe was one of the highlights of the year for me in 1990. Compuserve is a public-access information network. Anyone with a computer modem can connect any time. Sports Forum is a special place in Compuserve, where you can find hundreds of Rotisserie people [they call it FBB] on line, humming and chattering away all year round.

All you have to do is connect to CompuServe. Any computer store can give you complete information, everything you need. You can sign on right now. Just connect to CompuServe, and when you get the "!" prompt, type "GO FANS" and you're in. What can you do when you're in? All kinds of neat stuff. Some of my favorites last year:

• Play in a league, or two. At any time, you can look over the rosters and standings of dozens of leagues. Before the season starts, you can select one of the rosters abandoned by the bozo who mangled it last year; with a core of gem players and a fistful of fantasy money, you can go to auction and turn your franchise around. If rehab projects aren't your specialty, you can join one of the many new leagues that form every spring.

Since 1990 I have been playing in one American League and one National League on CompuServe. Every year, the sharks came swarming to feast on poor, helpless Benson. So far, I have done OK: Two first place teams in two years in the NL, One first place and one third place after two years in the AL. Even if you don't want to play, you can be a spectator, and follow my agony every step of the way; it's all there for public viewing

The Forum staff provides a highly professional, unique service combining timely stats with league secretarial, commissioner, and social services. The competition is only as serious as you want to make it. It's fun, fun, fun.

HIGHLY RECOMMENDED BOOKS

THE ROTISSERIE BASEBALL ANNUAL
by John Benson

Every year, John produces this unique book. Fifty scouts and writers nationwide cover every player on every team, down to the Double-A level. Who's going to play and how well they are going to do. The most complete, most up-to-date, best informed outlook you can find anywhere, all uniquely tailored to suit the needs of people just like you.

You receive complete forecast stats for the coming year and dollar values for every player. Not backward-looking, calculated dollar values for past performance, but current dollar values for the coming season.

You find numerous essays on the latest techniques in drafting, bidding, managing your roster and scouting talent at all levels from the game's top writers and analysts.

If you can afford to allow your opponents to keep an edge over you, go right ahead. But if you want to make sure that your arsenal is just as full as the other owners, then you need the current book.

Back issues are available along with the current edition ($22.95) from Devyn Press, 800-274-2221. (See the order form on the last page of this book.)

ROTISSERIE® BASEBALL: A TO Z
by John Benson

Every player you need to know, from Abare to Zurn. It includes hundreds of minor leagers, scuting reports, projected stats and $ values. Your desktop "Who's Who." What's happening in each player's career? What's the outlook for the upcoming season? Over 1400 players previewed.

$15.95 Call Devyn Press at 1-800-274-2221 to order.

10 OTHER HIGHLY-RECOMMENDED ROTISSERIE BOOKS

1. Glen Waggoner's ROTISSERIE® LEAGUE BASEBALL: THE OFFICIAL RULEBOOK AND DRAFT DAY GUIDE (Available at your favorite bookstore)

2. Peter Golenbock's HOW TO WIN AT ROTISSERIE® BASEBALL (Available at your favorite bookstore)

3. Bill James' THE BASEBALL BOOK (Available at your favorite bookstore)

4. STATS MINOR LEAGUE HANDBOOK (1-800-637-8287)

5. STATS MAJOR LEAGUE HANDBOOK (1-800-637-8287)

6. STATS PLAYER PROFILES (1-800-637-8287)

7. THE SPORTING NEWS BASEBALL REGISTER (1-800-825-8508)

8. THE SPORTING NEWS FANTASY BASEBALL OWNER'S MANUAL (1-800-825-8508)

9. Mike Gimbel's BASEBALL PLAYER & TEAM RATINGS (1-800-835-0220)

10. BASEBALL AMERICA'S DIRECTORY (1-800-845-2726)

ROTISSERIE® BASEBALL:
PLAYING FOR BLOOD
by John Benson and Randall Baron

This is the long-awaited 2ND VOLUME OF OUR SERIES (PLAYING FOR FUN IS VOLUME 1). Playing for Blood is for advanced to expert players and includes all the serious subjects that are crucial for winning in the most competitive leagues. It is available for $12.95 from Devyn Press, 1-800-274-2221 (see the order form on the last page of this book.)

The following are chapters in PLAYING FOR BLOOD:

PART I: VALUATION

    1st Inning — Valuation Concepts

    2nd Inning — Hitters' Dollar Valuation

    3rd Inning — Pitchers' Dollar Valuation

    4th Inning — Dollar Value "Adjustments"

PART II: THE DRAFT OR AUCTION

    5th Inning — Optimal Bidding

    6th Inning — Draft Price Inflation

    7th Inning — Auction Budgeting

PART III: ROSTER MANAGEMENT

    8th Inning — Dealing with Injuries

    9th Inning — Fair Trading

    10th Inning — Trading Tactics: Don't Try to Look Too Smart

    11th Inning — Winter Moves You Should Make

PART IV: ADVANCED SCOUTING

    12th Inning — Watch What Managers Do, Not What They Say

    13th Inning — Minor League Notebook

    14th Inning — Prospects and Suspects: The Politics of Playing Time

    15th Inning — In Search of a Level Playing Field

    16th Inning — Competitive Intelligence

    17th Inning — Psychological Warfare

APPENDIX

For your convenience, we have repeated the 25 rule choices for your league which are found throughout the book. You may use this as a starting check list and add others as you wish. By having them all in one section, it will be easier for you to fill in your preferences. You can make copies for all of the owners if you meet for a rules discussion or vote. The page where each topic is found in the book is indicated.

Page 21

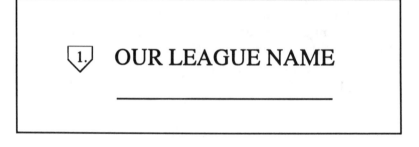

Page 22

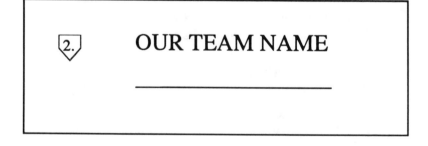

We have indicated our recommended choices for rules throughout the book by *.

Page 31

3. The positions for our league are:

A)	☐ 2 Catchers*	☐ Other _____
B)	☐ 1 1B*	☐ Other _____
C)	☐ 1 2B*	☐ Other _____
D)	☐ 1 3B*	☐ Other _____
E)	☐ 1 SS*	☐ Other _____
F)	☐ 1 Middle Inf (2B or SS)*	☐ Other _____
G)	☐ 1 Corner Inf (1B or 3B)*	☐ Other _____
H)	☐ 5 OF*	☐ Other _____
I)	☐ 1 Extra Hitter (any position)*	☐ Other _____
J)	☐ 9 Pitchers*	☐ Other _____

4. The total number of active players per team (add the positions above) is:

☐ 23*
☐ Other_____

5. The pitchers may be

☐ any number of starters and relievers*
☐ Other_____

6. The number of teams in our league is:

- [ ] 8
- [ ] 9
- [ ] 10
- [ ] 11
- [ ] 12*
- [ ] Other_____

7. Players are used from:

- [ ] *NL only
- [ ] *AL only
- [ ] Both Leagues

8. Will the league have a Reserve List? (See page 29 for a further discussion.) [ ] Yes* [ ] No

If yes, how many players on the RL?_____

If yes, when will the players be chosen?_____

9. Will the league have a Farm System?

[ ] Yes [ ] No

If yes, how many players in the FS?_____

If yes, when will the players be chosen?_____

10. Our league will have
- [ ] 8*   catagories.
- [ ] 9
- [ ] 10
- [ ] Other_____

Catagories

11. Standard:
- [ ] BA
- [ ] HR
- [ ] RBI
- [ ] SB

- [ ] R
- [ ] IP
- [ ] OBP
- [ ] NSB
- [ ] K

- [ ] W
- [ ] S
- [ ] ERA
- [ ] BPI

- [ ] WL%
- [ ] E
- [ ] F%
- [ ] Other _____

12. Is there a minimum number of IP per team?
Yes [ ]   No [ ]

If yes, what is the penalty if the team does not meet the requirements?_____
_____

Page 42

13. Our league will use the ☐ standard*
☐ one-dimensional method
of scoring.

14. Who will keep our stats?

☐ Stat service*   Name _____
☐ Someone in league Name _____
☐ Non-owner   Name _____

Page 47

15. Our ☐ draft or ☐ auction will be held on_____.
It will be   ☐ at a meeting
☐ by phone.

Page 63

16. Our league will allow roster moves
☐ when a player is formally placed on the DL by his team
☐ RLBA rules
☐ Other (why) _____

17. A. We will allow _____
    (how many) free roster moves.

    B. We will allow _____
    (how many) roster moves that cost _____ each.

18. A. Free agent drafts will be held
    - [ ] weekly
    - [ ] every 2 weeks
    - [ ] monthly
    - [ ] never
    - [ ] other _____

    B. The free agent draft will be held
    - [ ] at a meeting
    - [ ] by phone

19. Will our league have a "grace period?"
    Yes [ ] No [ ] If yes, until what date? _____

20. Will we allow unlimited "free" roster moves?
Yes ☐ No ☐ If yes, until what date? _____

21. We will allow _____ free
agent acquisitions in September.
The date _____
The cost _____ .

22. Trading Policy:

Yes ☐ No* ☐ A: Teams are allowed to make trades of any
kind throughout the year.

B: Teams are allowed to make trades with the following
restrictions:

Yes* ☐ No ☐ From July 31 — August 31, trades may take
place only between teams next to each
other in the preceding week's standings.

Yes* ☐ No ☐ From September 1 — end of the season, no
trades are allowed.

Yes* ☐ No ☐ Trades must be made position for position (P +
OF for P + OF) during the season.

Trades made in the off season are ☐ bound ☐ not bound* by the position requirements.

Trades ☐ change ☐ do not change salaries of players. Explain any changes. _____

_____

Trades ☐ do ☐ do not affect the contract status of players.

Yes* ☐ No ☐ Trades prohibit "players to be named later" and "future considerations."

Yes* ☐ No ☐ Trades are subject to the anti-dumping rules in the official Rotisserie rules. See the book.

Yes* ☐ No ☐ Trades must be for the same number of players (1 for 1, 2 for 2, etc.)

23. Trades are subject to a fee of _____.

24. Retentions

Our league ☐ will ☐ will not have player retentions each year.

If we will have retentions:

A. Each team may keep up to _____ players. Further explanation if the team's position in the previous season or some other reason allows varying the number of retentions for each team _____

_____
_____

B. There is a requirement to keep at least _____ players per team. Further explanation (if necessary) _____
_____

C. Retained players must be: ☐ given to ☐ phoned in to ☐ FAXed to ☐ other _____ (name of secretary, commissioner or other responsible person) by _____ (time and date).

D. Other information required to be given to the person in C. above:
☐ salary (if you use the auction method)
☐ length of contract
Other_____

_____

198

E. Players may be retained for up to _____ years. Further explanation (if necessary) _____

_____

_____

F. We will have Toppers' Rights (see page 94) on players ☐ Yes ☐ No. If yes, they are available after _____ years and they can be kept for _____ years.

25. Salaries

A. A retained player will have the following salary:

_____

_____

_____

_____

B. Salaries of various acquistions:
   Traded players during the season _____
   Traded player during the off season _____
   Free agent _____
   Minor leaguer acquired during the season _____
   Player brought up from the Reserve list or
       farm system _____
   Player who comes over from the Other League (AL to NL
       or NL to AL) during the season_____
   Other _____

       _____

       _____

199

DEVYN PRESS ORDER FORM

Title	Quantity	Price	Total
Rotisserie Baseball—Playing For Fun—Volume 1 by John Benson and Randall Baron All the essentials of getting organized and playing smart		$12.95	
Rotisserie Baseball-Playing for Blood—Volume 2 by John Benson and Randall Baron All the serious information, valuation, auction economics and roster management		$12.95	
The Rotisserie Baseball Annual, by John Benson The biggest, most serious, most in-depth preview of the coming season.		$22.95	
Rotisserie Baseball A to Z, by John Benson Your complete player guide and who's who		$15.95	

Back issues of the
Rotisserie Baseball Annual
by John Benson
(Call for prices and availability)

	TOTAL (Before Shipping Added)	
	Add Shipping (See Chart)	
	Add KY. Sales Tax (If Necessary)	
	AMOUNT ENCLOSED	

U.S. SHIPPING CHARGES

	UPS	EXPRESS
1 BOOK	$3.95	$10.25
2 BOOKS	$5.95	$12.75
3 or more BOOKS	$7.95	$14.50

DEVYN PRESS
3600 Chamberlain Lane
Suite 230
Louisville, KY 40241

IN THE U.S. AND CANADA
CALL TOLL FREE
1-800-274-2221
ANYTIME.
FAX 502-426-2044

NAME _____

ADDRESS _____

CITY, STATE, ZIP _____

DAYTIME PHONE _____

PLEASE INDICATE METHOD OF PAYMENT _____ VISA _____ M/C _____ CHECK

VISA / M/C NUMBER _____

EXP. DATE _____

YOU MAY SEND A FAX OR LEAVE AN
ORDER ON OUR VOICE MAIL ANYTIME.

Rotisserie League Baseball is a registered trademark of R.L.B.A., Inc.